Experiencing Joy

Experiencing Joy

A 30 Day Devotional Journey

Ruth Teakle
& a Company of Friends

EXPERIENCING JOY
Copyright © 2022 by Ruth Teakle

All rights reserved. Neither this publication nor any part of this publication may be reproduced or transmitted in any form or by any means, electronic or mechanical, including photocopying, recording or any information storage and retrieval system, without permission in writing from the author.

Unless otherwise indicated, scripture quotations are taken from the Holy Bible, NEW INTERNATIONAL VERSION®, NIV® Copyright © 1973, 1978, 1984, 2011 by Biblica, Inc.® Used by permission. All rights reserved worldwide. Scripture quotations marked (AMP) are taken from the Amplified® Bible, Copyright © 1954, 1958, 1962, 1964, 1965, 1987 by The Lockman Foundation. Used by permission. Scripture quotations marked (ESV) are taken from The Holy Bible, English Standard Version® (ESV®), copyright © 2001 by Crossway, a publishing ministry of Good News Publishers. Used by permission. All rights reserved. Scripture quotations marked (NKJV) are taken from the New King James Version®. Copyright © 1982 by Thomas Nelson, Inc. Used by permission. All rights reserved. Scripture quotations marked (NLT) are taken from the Holy Bible, New Living Translation, copyright ©1996, 2004, 2007 by Tyndale House Foundation. Used by permission of Tyndale House Publishers, Inc., Carol Stream, Illinois 60188. All rights reserved. Scripture quotations marked (TPT) are taken from The Passion Translation®. Copyright © 2017, 2018 by Passion & Fire Ministries, Inc. Used by permission. All rights reserved. ThePassionTranslation.com. Scripture quotations marked (NASB) are taken from the New American Standard Bible®, Copyright © 1960, 1962, 1963, 1968, 1971, 1972, 1973, 1975, 1977, 1995 by The Lockman Foundation. Used by permission. Scripture quotations marked (TLB) are taken from The Living Bible copyright © 1971 by Tyndale House Foundation. Used by permission of Tyndale House Publishers Inc., Carol Stream, Illinois 60188. All rights reserved. The Living Bible, TLB, and the The Living Bible logo are registered trademarks of Tyndale House Publishers. Scripture quotations marked (Phillips) are taken from The New Testament in Modern English by J.B Phillips copyright © 1960, 1972 J. B. Phillips. Administered by The Archbishops' Council of the Church of England. Used by Permission. Scripture quotations marked (VOICE) are taken from The Voice™. Copyright © 2008 by Ecclesia Bible Society. Used by permission. All rights reserved. Scripture quotations marked (NET) are taken from The NET Bible® second edition, copyright ©1996-2017 all rights reserved. Scripture quotations marked (CEV) are from the Contemporary English Version Copyright © 1991, 1992, 1995 by American Bible Society. Used by Permission. Scripture quotations marked (HCSB) are taken from the Holman Christian Standard Bible®, Used by Permission HCSB ©1999,2000,2002,2003,2009 Holman Bible Publishers. Holman Christian Standard Bible®, Holman CSB®, and HCSB® are federally registered trademarks of Holman Bible Publishers. Scripture quotations marked (CEB) from the COMMON ENGLISH BIBLE. © Copyright 2011 COMMON ENGLISH BIBLE. All rights reserved. Used by permission. (www.CommonEnglishBible.com).

Print ISBN: 978-1-4866-2301-3
eBook ISBN: 978-1-4866-2302-0

Word Alive Press
119 De Baets Street, Winnipeg, MB R2J 3R9
www.wordalivepress.ca

Cataloguing in Publication may be obtained through Library and Archives Canada

Contents

Preface:	Getting Started	xi
Day 1:	Sunporch Joy	1
Day 2:	The Joy of Community	3
Day 3:	The Joy of Salvation	5
Day 4:	Stay Focused	7
Day 5:	Finding True Joy	9
Day 6:	The Sound of Joy	11
Day 7:	The Joy of Intercession	13
Day 8:	Joy in the Journey	15
Day 9:	A Joyful Welcome	17
Day 10:	Joy and Strength	19
Day 11:	Embracing Surrender	21
Day 12:	A Father's Joy	23
Day 13:	The Joyful News	25
Day 14:	Joyful Praise	27
Day 15:	Morning Is Coming	29
Day 16:	In His Presence	31
Day 17:	Joy Trumps Them All	33
Day 18:	Joy Challenged	35
Day 19:	Knowing His Voice	37
Day 20:	Hannah's Joy	39
Day 21:	Liberating Joy	41
Day 22:	Ridiculous Joy	43
Day 23:	The King's Delight	45
Day 24:	The Joy of Protection	47
Day 25:	A Joy-Filled Knowing	49

Day 26:	The Joy of Generosity	51
Day 27:	Jumping for Joy!	53
Day 28:	Joy in Suffering?	55
Day 29:	The Practice of Joy	57
Day 30:	Six Biblical Habits to Help Cultivate Joy	59
	Small Group Helps	63
	Discussion Questions	65
	Contributors	73
	About the Author	81

This devotional, *Experiencing Joy*, is dedicated with tons of love
to a very dear friend and intercessor,
Gladys M. Reardon,
who in her 91st year continues to experience and epitomize
unrestricted
JOY
like few I have known.
Her life is a colourful canvas of the true character of a joy-filled saint.
Consistently loving,
Laughter filled,
Ungrudgingly generous,
Uncomplicated,
Brave hearted,
Battle ready,
Undeterred by pain,
Eternity focused,
Passionately committed,
Lover of Jesus.

Getting Started

But the fruit produced by the Holy Spirit within you is divine love in all its varied expressions: joy that overflows, *peace that subdues, patience that endures, kindness in action, a life full of virtue, faith that prevails, gentleness of heart, and strength of spirit . . . they are meant to be limitless.*
—Galatians 5:22–23a, TPT (emphasis added)

God has invaded our world with good news of great joy for all people. What would it mean to really grasp His majesty, grace, love, and presence in our lives? One of the first expressions of His divine love within is a joy that overflows. Joy—love rejoicing! The more we come to know God, the more we experience the source of all joy.

Jesus said, *"If you remain in me and I in you, you will bear much fruit . . ."* (John 15:5b). If we're connected to Jesus, then joy should be evident in our lives. As a branch joined to Jesus, the life-giving vine, the fruit we bear should be joyful! When we truly abide in Him, we will know the fullness of His joy.

Most of us prefer to live out our days happy. We might describe the feeling or experience of happiness as one of bliss, cheer, satisfaction, contentment, lightheartedness, or freedom from trouble. As we press in to discover biblical joy, we aren't throwing happiness or the joys of life to the curb. These are wonderful! However, sometimes we face situations that threaten our attempt to live out our lives in joy. It might be a health problem, a rejection, financial strain, a relational conflict, or anxiety about wars and uncertainty across the globe. With one event, one thought, one word, joy can slip from our grasp if we're not well connected to its source.

We were made for joy, to be recipients and then distributors. These daily devotionals are offered to invite you to engage with the testimonies of those who have found the true source of joy—people from the neighbourhood of believers with real stories, some even with personal obstacles to joy. As well, you will revisit the lives of men and women from the Bible who experienced great victories and learned some lasting lessons about joy in their lifetimes. They will encourage you to cultivate a consistent *biblical joy* that isn't based on circumstance. They'll remind you of some life-changing promises and commands from God's Word that you can apply in your own life.

If you find that your joy has been depleted or abandoned due to circumstances or choices, you have selected the right journey for these next thirty days. I believe God will meet you here and restore what is rightly yours as a child of God—an inheritance that He has promised. Press in to know Him in a deeper way, regain your focus, and embrace His presence. Together, let's welcome a fresh experience of His joy.

Sunporch Joy

Day One

... You direct me on the path that leads to a beautiful life. As I walk with You ... I know true joy and contentment.

—Psalm 16:11, VOICE

The old Singer sewing machine was seldom idle. It was dedicated to the cause—that is, the cause of Christ. Day after day, the pedal would rise and fall with the pressure of her foot. The re-filled bobbin would remain ready to tackle zippers, hems, or the formation of little girls' dresses out of discarded men's ties. Early in the morning or late into the night, you could find her sewing in the sunporch.

From the time I was very young, I watched my mother restore donated garments and repurpose them for those in need. It fascinated me so much that one day, around the age of eight, I tried to help while Mom was out of the room. My index finger still tells the tale of my adventure with the needle.

Hundreds of boxes of adult clothing were earmarked for the Scott Mission in Toronto, while the heavier winter clothing and children's items were restored and allocated to the Spillenars in northern Ontario.

On top of this ongoing project that lasted well into her seventies, it was her delight to mend or alter garments for her family and friends. Formal training wasn't needed—she was gifted. She seldom made a mistake. The only one of any consequence was the day my sister-in-law had Mom shorten and hem a new pair of Levi's. Partway through, Mom was called to prepare dinner, and the distraction took its toll. She returned to her cutting and hemming, accidentally shortening the same leg she had already finished. Definitely a new look!

Mom's life was humble but stressful. She had plenty of reasons to be more burdened than joyful. I was the first child, born when she was thirty-seven. The three boys that followed demanded more attention. (They would plead guilty as charged.) It was a constant race to keep us all out of trouble. But caring for people never just meant looking after us; her picture was broader. She was moved by compassion and knew the joy that came with serving God through loving others in practical ways.

Affirmation and appreciation weren't readily offered at home for all Mom did, but when she found her spot at that sewing machine, her joy and contentment were complete. It was many years before I realized that other than when she was on her knees at the end of the day, this was the place where she found joy in His presence. She could shut out the clamour, the harsh words, the concerns about lack, and the uncertainties about her personal health. It was at the old treadle sewing machine that she had a vision for the needs of others, which included her obedience to God's call to become part of the solution.

When happiness dissipates and circumstances are challenging, joy remains if you see what Heaven sees. It's a joy that grows by the working of the Holy Spirit in a life, and that's how it was for Mom. Every new project brought her joy. Each additional donation left at her door was a reason to celebrate. When the transport truck driver would stop by to pick up the dozens of boxes that were ready and packed, she would beam with delight. There was no set schedule. They would just come when they had some empty space on a truck. I think that was part of the joy—the anticipation of the fulfilment of Heaven's most recent assignment.

Lesson learned! True joy is birthed out of a relationship with the eternal. Joy and contentment can be found at kitchen sinks, in rocking chairs, in workshops, or in sunporches ... if we'll allow ourselves to be led by the Spirit of God.

Father, help me to embrace the joy of the simple things and the familiar places. Guide me in the seemingly small tasks you call me to do that are really an invitation to experience that joy!

The Joy of Community

Day Two

fulfill my joy... having the same love, being of one accord, of one mind. Let nothing be done through selfish ambition or conceit ... Let each of you look out not only for his own interests, but also for the interests of others.
—Philippians 2:2–4, NKJV

Paul's letter to the Philippians is commonly known as the letter of joy. With the salvation of Lydia, and later the Philippian jailer and his family, the church at Philippi had begun. As the church grew, Paul visited them and gained a heartfelt, God-given connection. (This means they were probably his favourites.)

Paul's relationship with the Philippian church is well-seasoned with gratitude and prayer. He cares deeply for them—that much is evident throughout the letter. He unpacks for them (and for us) what it means to follow Jesus in day-to-day life. He emphasizes that one of the key aspects of life with Jesus is His people—the church. This letter gives us a glimpse into healthy Christian community fueled by love. Paul expresses how much they've been in his thoughts and prayers, even when he has been suffering. (After all, he's writing from jail!) He's clear on the value of their support and prays for them with great insight and hope.

We too are designed for relationship. Our Christian community is meant to help us grow our relationships to the point where we're as prayerful and as joyful as Paul is in this letter. Through the body of Christ, relationships can become transformational in our walk with God.

Experiencing Joy

Our God-given hunger for relationship has made two years of COVID-19 lockdowns very challenging. Coming together as a church family would normally provide opportunities to serve, love, grow, and pray together. We've had to work with a supernatural creativity to reach out to communities and mission fields in need of the gospel during this time. While technology has proved to be a powerful tool, we've desperately missed the kind of close fellowship with which we're most familiar.

When we experience biblical joy, especially within "the body," we know a work of the Holy Spirit is happening in our hearts. Paul demonstrates, however, that joy and sacrifice often go hand-in-hand. Threaded into the tapestry of his letter, Paul reminds the church that love, faith, and even joy can not only survive in difficult circumstances, but they can thrive. We can still discover and experience joy when life seems to be restrained by mandates, masks, scientific data, or political preferences. However, if we choose to withdraw from others because of differing views, or resent leaders who haven't done things "our way," we diminish our opportunity for joy, because we're called to do life together and be "one body."

As I write this devotional, we're on the verge of community once again. I can feel my heart ready to burst that we'll see each other smile, share a hug or a cup of coffee, and "Amen" the pastor's message. And all in the same room at the same time! From a distance, I can hear the thrill of uproarious worship and envision the fabulous spread of a shared meal in the church gym.

Lydia and the Philippian jailer had little in common before they followed Jesus. He became their "one thing," and they were able to walk together. May I suggest that we each do our part in submitting any frustrations felt or judgements made in a past season to our loving Heavenly Father, so that we can walk together in peace and in the power of the Holy Spirit as we resume Christian community. Let's make Him our one thing as we build, in joy, together.

Jesus, I am committing to set my opinions and preferences aside in order to be a vessel of your peace and a carrier of your joy to those around me. In your name. Amen.

The Joy of Salvation

Day Three
Contributed by Betty Chisholm

With joy you will draw water from the wells of salvation.

—Isaiah 12:3

The Lord has always tugged at my heart to reach beyond the obvious sites for ministry. In our first year as Christians, John and I made our first visit to a detention centre, where I sang and shared my testimony. That visit began a lifelong investment in sharing Jesus in some very humbling yet powerful ways—and leading people to Him became one of my greatest joys in life.

Every visit was unique and unpredictable, but I recall the first time we were permitted to go up to the Levels to hold our service. There was trouble in one of the pods with shouting and scuffling, and the guards had been called. One of the inmates, named "R"—one giant of a young man—was the cause of the big disturbance. He was out of control but wanted to come to our service. He'd almost started a riot earlier and was now confined to a cell by himself. He was screaming like a madman, especially at the correction officers.

I had a lot of faith and enthusiasm in those early days of my walk with God, but not a lot of experience or wisdom, so I asked the correction officers to let him come. They said it was much too risky. I told the guards that the music might calm him down, but he continued to disrupt. Finally, in an effort to settle him, they agreed to let him come in with the promise of being a "good boy." By the time they had made that decision, I had already stopped singing and had shared my testimony, with an overwhelming and powerful response to the salvation call.

Experiencing Joy

Seeing "R" coming, I began wondering what deadly can of worms I had opened. But despite all the confusion and noise, I sensed a strong presence of God in the room. Nothing was going to steal my joy or the joy of those newly committed Kingdom sons. They had all prayed, and some were even weeping. As the guards unlocked the door, one of them said with a smirk, "Good luck with this one; you got your wish." Then he walked away, obviously relieved.

With my shoulders back and my eyes fixed on his, I stopped this towering, seething giant at the door and said, "You can't take another step unless you're here to sincerely pray like these guys just did." The scene replicated that of the Roadrunner meeting the Hulk! What? I could hardly believe what had just come out of my mouth. A look at the other guys in the room clued me in that I was not alone in my shock.

"R" looked down at me from his massive, muscular six-foot-four frame and then turned to the others. "Did you guys pray like she was telling you?" The response was a resounding, "Yes." To my amazement, he got down on his knees right there, in front of everyone, with guards still watching. I briefly summarized the message of salvation and asked, "Are you ready to receive Jesus today, right now?" His body language said it all. "Yes," he replied, now settled and in his right mind. Heaven gained another recruit that day as a very humbled big "R" allowed Jesus to give him a fresh start.

My heart was bursting! I had just tasted again the joy that Heaven feels when a sinner repents. Our ministry in prisons has continued for over thirty-five years, with hundreds of salvations—each one releasing in me that wonderful joy from the Spirit of God. Friends, the fields are ready for harvest. Ask God to fan the flame in you that will lead others to experience the joy of His salvation through you.

> *I rejoice today, Holy Spirit, in your power to work in the most unusual ways, if only we are obedient. I pray that a new boldness and hunger will be imparted to me to see others experience the joy of your salvation and be transformed by your love.*

Stay Focused

Day Four

> *... let us run with endurance the race that is set before us, looking unto Jesus, the author and finisher of our faith, who for the joy that was set before Him endured the cross ...*
>
> —Hebrews 12:1b–2, NKJV

Running a race always means avoiding distractions, seeing the end goal, and being motivated by what's ahead. For a disciple of Jesus, our goal is to keep our eyes on Him, to hold an unhindered gaze on the "author and finisher" of our faith. If we lose focus, we may settle for easy circumstances with temporary pleasures. Losing focus also makes the painful and difficult events seem like ends in themselves, with no hope of experiencing anything more than disappointment and defeat.

I vividly remember carrying and giving birth to my children. Every detail seems like it happened yesterday. Each child was anticipated and welcomed, *but* the pregnancies and births were unnerving, peppered with moments of anxiety, surrounded with pain and uncertainty. For the first six months, I wondered if I'd ever be able to hold down food again. Then at nine months it was "Could someone please get this baby out *now*?" and "Why isn't the doctor here yet?" It's a wonder to many how a mother can go through all of this and within thirty seconds of the baby being placed on her chest be smiling ear to ear while Dad snaps photos. Does this make sense?

The answer is yes. What makes all of it manageable is the focus on what's ahead. Yes, there's also joy in the journey. None of us enjoy the pain that's involved, but there's always strength to endure because we stay focused on the promise. We don't have to wait for its fulfilment to begin to experience the joy. We see it already with eyes of faith: the blessing of new life, Heaven's plan. The baby laid across the chest is relief, pleasure, satisfaction, awe—and often an outpouring of tears of deep joy.

Hebrews 12:1–2 says that Jesus found joy even while enduring horrific pain and humiliation: *"who for the joy that was set before Him endured the cross"* (ESV). This is one of the greatest paradoxes of all time. How could Jesus, while hanging on a cross, have experienced any joy at all? One of the most brutal, excruciating execution methods of all time left little room for anything but agony, distress, pain, and heartache. There was nothing in His immediate situation that called for joy. He didn't find joy or pleasure in the nails that were driven into His hands, or the crown of thorns that encircled the ruptured skin across His head. He didn't find joy in carrying the cross or in the degrading and demoralizing words spoken against Him. *But He was strengthened to endure because of the joy in the guaranteed outcome.*

God allowed Him to see that the price He had to pay would buy us back, and that joy kept Him on the cross. When He looked into His Father's eyes, He was filled with the assurance that this act would reunite a lost humanity to Him, both now and in the age to come. With that focus, He glimpsed into the future and saw that because of the cross, we would gain restored sonship and identity.

The more time we take to learn what God has revealed about what He has prepared for us, the more joy we'll find in that hope. The basis of our joy is the confidence that regardless of what's going on around us, God loves us and is our source. It doesn't always make sense in the natural, but we can run with endurance and strength in the darkest circumstance or the greatest need if our eyes remain focused on Him.

> *Jesus, you are my source and my strength. I let go of the distractions and reset my focus on you. You have placed eternity in my heart. The hope I have in you restores my joy and brings me peace.*

Finding True Joy

Day Five

Contributed by Christopher Collins

Those who have been ransomed by the Lord ... will be filled with joy and gladness.

—Isaiah 35:10, NLT

As the youngest of three, I wanted for nothing. I was abundantly spoiled. I grew up with a misguided belief that I was exceptionally good, maybe even a cut above, and this poorly calculated assessment of myself meant I was entitled. Life was good. At the age of nineteen, I took this belief system with me to an altar and "added" Jesus to my life. He was the "supplement" who would make my good life even better. Life was all about me.

When I fell in love, I was young, immature, self-focused, and indulging in all the "must haves" but having no real joy. I was still living under the belief that I should get whatever I wanted, and when the disappointments were undeniable and the debt became unmanageable, I was angry with God.

Ten years into the marriage, my wife became suicidal and on two occasions attempted to take my life in a murder/suicide attempt. This was the final straw. This was not the "good life" God had promised. I ran! I ran right into the arms of another woman and to the comfort of alcohol and pornography. I ran to whatever I thought would give me pleasure. I left the church, divorced my wife, and didn't look back.

Three years of wandering went by, and nothing in my life made me happy. The things I looked to for happiness were bringing me nothing but pain. I woke up one Christmas morning alone in my apartment thinking, *Is this the rest of my life? Living alone and empty?* And there in my brokenness, God reached me. My eyes were opened. I saw that I was far from good—I was sinful, selfish, and hollow. I remember going to my car, placing my head on the steering wheel, and crying out to God. "Lord, if this is you, please let me know."

I arrived at work that day and was stopped by a co-worker outside. "Please don't think I'm weird, but I'm a Christian, and God wants you to know that He loves you and wants you to have this." She handed me a mix tape (yes, I'm that old) of worship songs and some words of encouragement and scripture. I drove around for hours that night listening to the music and crying, overwhelmed by the sense of God's love for me. For the first time, I finally got it! Jesus doesn't make a bad life good or a good life better. Jesus takes a life that is dead in sin and brings it to life through Him! I pulled my car over to a quiet place and surrendered my life completely to Jesus. In that moment, He became my joy—pure, unhindered, sweet—and my previously entitled heart felt serious gratitude.

I began going to church and drew closer to God through worship, prayer, and *really* reading the Bible for the first time! His Word became "... *a joy and the delight of my heart...*" (Jeremiah 15:16, ESV). I had finally found real joy, but it wasn't in acquiring material things or indulging my appetite for sin. It was found in Jesus and in knowing that I had been called by His name! Once I realized He was all I needed, I trusted Him to heal me in every area of my life, and Heaven's joy rained down over my life. I wasn't looking for anything, just loving God, when He placed a beautiful woman of God in my life. Nancy, His gift, and I have been married now for twenty-one years, and we're loving and serving Him together. And yes, the ransomed of the Lord cannot help but be filled with His joy!

Jesus, I'm filled with joy and gladness in your love. Forgive me for the times I supplemented my own selfish desires with your goodness. You paid a high price for my salvation, and I am grateful and blessed.

The Sound of Joy

Day Six

He will yet fill your mouth with laughter and your lips with shouts of joy.
—Job 8:21

As a child, I often found joy in the most unusual and stressful circumstances that gave my parents reason for neither laughter nor celebration. I can't think of many things I did that annoyed my father more than laughing at my parents' serious and generally unsolvable problems. Immediately after I had unwittingly released the first snicker, one of my three devious brothers would be ready to help perpetrate my demise with funny faces or pokes to cause a full explosion of merriment. I remember many times being sent to my room for not stopping my laughter when I was instructed to do so. I'd have to bury my face in my pillow and hope that my father didn't hear me during the continuing hilarity.

It's not that my father didn't find his own moments of laughter. His repertoire of recycled jokes would bring him a great gusto of laughter, whether it was the first time he told one or the twentieth. I think what he failed to realize, though, was that we are meant to be a people of joy! Some things just aren't worth the worry we give them! Laughter is simply uncontained joy. Many generations before us, God set up a foundation of joy and laughter in His covenant with Abraham and Sarah—and here we are, all these generations later, still defined by our roots. Let's look back.

When Abraham was almost one hundred, the Lord appeared to him and said that He would make a covenant with him and make him the father of many nations. He promised to make him fruitful and said that the covenant would be an everlasting covenant for all of the descendants and generations to come. This would happen through his wife, Sarah, who would be blessed with his son, and she would be the mother of nations. Abraham could hardly believe his ears. He fell on his face and laughed. Would Sarah have a child at the age of ninety? But God assured him that it would happen. When Sarah overheard the news, she laughed as she thought to herself, *Since I'm worn out and my husband is this old, will I really have this pleasure now?* The Lord reminded Abraham that nothing was too difficult for Him.

When their son came according to God's promise, they named him Isaac (the Hebrew for "laughter"). They wouldn't forget the story of Isaac's conception and birth. Every time Sarah looked at her son, she'd be reminded of God's ability to do the impossible, and her ability to do the impossible with God's strength. Laughter still reminds us of God's power and sovereignty to do what is beyond human comprehension. I suspect that neither Sarah nor Abraham's laughter (or hint of skepticism) was an offence to God. It's what you do when you're surprised by a joy so intense and overwhelming that all you can do is burst out laughing.[1]

Laughter is part of God's healing gift to each of us—as the Bible says, it's great medicine. It can boost the immune system and reduce blood pressure. It can relieve tension and alleviate stress. It can relax the muscles and uplift the soul. It can help to build connections with others and give us increased energy. A joyful heart is a delight to God. While joy does not negate our difficulties, disappointments, or sorrows, it nourishes the knowledge that God is present at every moment, and that gives us fresh hope.

I'm sure my dad is finding Heaven a suitable venue to share his jokes and perhaps even join in with the laughter of some friends. I pray that today you'd be provoked to laughter by the amazing truth of the incomprehensible gift of Jesus in your life. Laughter is the sound of joy.

> *Father, I am so glad that you have covenanted with us out of the truth that you can do the impossible. Help me to welcome opportunities for the healing power of laughter in my life.*

---

[1] Adapted from https://sermons.com/sermon/the-sound-of-joy/1492183.

The Joy of Intercession

Day Seven

Lord, in the morning you will hear me; in the morning I will present my case to you and then wait expectantly for an answer . . . may all who take shelter in you be happy. May they continually shout for joy.

—Psalm 5:3, 11, NET

Six women. Friday nights for two years. God-given friendships—a most treasured gift not easily replaced.

We met at the church to do business with Heaven. There was seldom a plan, just a great excitement that we knew we were going to meet with God. Sometimes we just sat in the church lobby in the dark, listening or occasionally weeping, for a long time before we prayed. At other times, we simply praised until we were ready. We might be on our knees with faces pressed against the wooden pews or walking the aisles with Bibles opened, declaring the Word. A favourite way to gather was seated in a circle in the church nursery. It didn't matter. They were undistracted sacred moments when we would link into His promises and His heart.

Every believer has the privilege of being used by God in effective intercession. Not just the favourite few. Not just the retired who find themselves with extra time. Not just people identified as "called" to the ministry of intercession. It's everyone's opportunity and one the six of us cherished. As we prayed for others, we understood more readily the love of God for our city, our nation, particular people groups, organizations, leaders, friends, and family members.

Experiencing Joy

We saw God move in situations above and far beyond our expectations. Two of the group saw their nominally Christian husbands begin relationships with God that far surpassed their dreams of possibility. We had regular reports of healings, restored relationships, and changed atmospheres. We joined faith with others in the city for broader requests.

Jesus was our great role model. He prayed for Peter, His friend, during times of severe testing and said this: *"Simon, Simon, Satan has asked to sift all of you as wheat. But I have prayed for you, Simon, that your faith may not fail"* (Luke 22:31–32a). Moses interceded for Aaron, his brother. Aaron had brought judgement on himself by making a golden calf for the people to worship. In Deuteronomy 9:20, we read, *"And the Lord was angry enough with Aaron to destroy him, but at that time I prayed for Aaron …"* Aaron's life was spared. Job learned the importance of praying for his friends after they misjudged him and failed to pray for him. As he forgave them, he called upon God for mercy to be released to them. As he did so, God blessed him with a double portion of what he had lost (Job 42:10).

Beyond the joy of answered prayer, we discovered an even greater gift. God had been bringing each of us into a deep, intimate place with Him, where we could truly experience His many expressions of love. At the end of our prayer time together, we often felt His presence heavy upon us, and it was hard to leave. We sensed His peace, His goodness, His kindness, and an unfamiliar depth of His joy. Psalm 16:11a says, *"You will make known to me the way of life; In Your presence is fullness of joy"* (NASB). In His sweet embrace, we experienced a sense of joy that transcended circumstance.

As intercessors, our work is to look ahead by faith to the good gifts God wants to give us and to agree with His plans according to His Word. A fresh outpouring of Heaven's joy comes from being in His presence and beholding His beauty. As we come near to Jesus in intercession, we can truly experience that joy!

Thank you, Heavenly Father, that Jesus has made the way for me to commune with you. Thank you for those sweet times in your presence when I can experience your love. Thank you for the privilege of intercession. I pray today that your will be done on earth as it is in Heaven.

Joy in the Journey

Day Eight
Contributed by Kayleigh Duggan

"Let your hope make you glad. Be patient in time of trouble and never stop praying."
—Romans 12:12, CEV

Four years on mission in Kenya and Tanzania. Check. The work of adjustment when returning to Canada completed. Check. A new focus in my church internship program. Check. My new-found freedom in discovering who I was and who God made me to be. Joy-filled and exciting!

Who could have predicted that a headache could change everything? Headaches come and go, and a little temporary pain relief usually solves the problem. But this nagging pain at the back of my head just wouldn't go away. After a few months with no answers or relief, I had some imaging done, and the news was shocking. A tumour was blocking almost all the spinal fluid in the fourth ventricle of my brain. On top of that, the medical community said that surgery on a tumour in this location wasn't an option, as the risks were too high. No pain medicine helped. Continuing with school or my part-time job, with no relief, seemed very unlikely.

My heart felt such confusion and disappointment, and I had many questions. Could God really be trusted? I *thought* He had assured me that He had a good plan for my life. Maybe I wouldn't even live to see it. Why wasn't He protecting me? With no sign of a solution, I needed a miracle.

By month seven (June), my family and I decided to look for other options, which led us to a hospital in Pittsburgh, Pennsylvania. The consultation confirmed some other surgical options with some very experienced and hopeful doctors. When the head neurosurgeon said, "I just have a gut feeling I can help you," I knew God was making a way. My joy in that moment was a bit like that of the woman who pushed through the crowd after twelve years of suffering to touch the hem of Jesus' robe. I hadn't even had the procedure, but my heart was already so full of hope. I saw a light at the end of the tunnel!

The $160,000 CAD price tag for the surgery, however, was out of reach. This next challenge was met by a whole community of supportive and faith-filled family, friends, and church members who partnered with the Sarah Tapley Foundation (https://www.facebook.com/sarahtapleyfoundation) to attempt to raise the funds. I believed with all my heart that God was in this surgery, and I had faith that the money would come in a timely manner. Within four weeks, the goal was exceeded! God's faithfulness was so clear. My joy found expression in my worship and times of thankful prayer.

A song played in my heart from the moment I woke up on the day of my surgery: "Closer than You Know" by Hillsong United. God was reminding me that He was right there with me. He worked His miracle through human hands, and when I woke up, the tumour was completely gone with no complications. I slowly regained all my strength in the weeks that followed.

Throughout the journey, I didn't know if God was going to instantaneously heal me, or if I'd have to wait years for a miracle, if I received one at all. At times the reports, helplessness, and setbacks eroded my joy. There was so much uncertainty, but God had a plan.

Today I am fully healed. My joy is growing! I'm back in school and internship, pursuing my dream of becoming a pastor. While I didn't welcome the pain, I've grown in trust and gratitude to Him, just for who He is. He showed me His faithfulness, and I rejoice in what He taught me in the journey. It is so precious. I wouldn't trade it for anything.

> *Jesus, help me in my journey to keep trusting when there is no good end in sight. Remind me of your goodness and faithfulness when my flesh is fighting to survive. I rest in you.*

A Joyful Welcome

Day Nine

Jesus ... went on ahead, going up to Jerusalem ... he sent two of his disciples, saying to them, "Go to the village ahead of you ... you will find a colt tied there, which no one has ever ridden. Untie it and bring it here ..." They brought it to Jesus, threw their cloaks on the colt and put Jesus on it ... When he came near the place ... the whole crowd of disciples began joyfully to praise God in loud voices for all the miracles they had seen: "Blessed is the king who comes in the name of the Lord!"

—Luke 19:28–38

Queen Elizabeth II's last visit to Canada came in the summer of 2010. For this well-travelled monarch, Canada was often her destination of choice for a royal tour. Her visits have included every province and territory. In 1970, accompanied by Prince Charles and Princess Anne, the Queen visited Manitoba for the one-hundredth anniversary of its entry into confederation. The visit was celebrated in pomp and splendour with gifts, presentations, speeches, and tributes. People flocked to see the royal entourage, and we were among them.

We waited in the blazing July sun until our skin was baked red for just a glimpse. Flags were waved, and significant police personnel paraded in front and behind. As she passed along with Prince Charles, this one of such distinction came within arm's reach! My heart raced as they paused and spoke to the people right beside us! The continuous clapping seemed most appropriate for such a dignitary. Every bystander along the roped-off passageway was in awe. Whispers, smiles, Canadian flags, and enthusiastic waves of joy were abundant. A welcome with obvious elements of detailed prestigious planning is to be expected for a sovereign.

I've often wondered what it would have been like to be part of the crowd that welcomed King Jesus as He entered Jerusalem. As He made His way from the Mount of Olives, delightful praise came from the grateful, believing multitude, their palm branches laid across the road before Him. The enthusiastic chorus echoed the angels' song at Bethlehem. He drew faith and admiration from His followers. They had tasted His grace and compassion, and they knew His miracles. Sadly, while the multitude praised, the Pharisees murmured.

In preparation for that entry, Jesus had sent for a colt, one that hadn't been ridden and that He could have on loan. It wasn't really becoming of a king to make his entry on a borrowed colt, attended by common men, honoured only with shouts of joy. Where was the convoy of soldiers, the trumpets, and the white stallion? While the crowd dreamed of a throne, He contemplated the cross. There was no doubt in the minds of the faithful that this Jesus was the Messiah, the heir to the throne of David. At last, thought His disciples, His hour had come—at last their long-delayed hopes were about to be fulfilled.

As He neared Jerusalem, however, He wept. He wasn't there for pomp and pageantry and worldly acclaim but to seek a sovereignty of another kind, one of a different realm altogether.

Today, our hosannas to the King aren't always as loud and as unified as that day when Jesus rode into Jerusalem. But they rise from little country churches, from hospital beds, from kitchen sinks, and from underground churches across the globe—songs of the redeemed, songs of gratitude, songs of strength and joy. As His subjects, we have the great privilege to rejoice in His goodness and majesty. And these praises are but a prelude to that day when the redeemed of every kindred and tribe will cast their crowns at His feet. He will receive the glory due His name. On that day, we will sing together a grand hallelujah of great joy!

Jesus, today, I release to you my hallelujahs! You are my Rock, my Redeemer, my Joy, my Saviour, and my soon-coming King! You are so worthy of my praise.

Joy and Strength

Day Ten

Contributed by Joy Slaughter

Then Nehemiah the governor, Ezra the priest and teacher of the Law, and the Levites who were instructing the people said to them all, "This day is holy to the Lord your God. Do not mourn or weep... for the joy of the Lord is your strength."
—Nehemiah 8:9, 10b

This past Christmas two colourful and fragrant candles were given to us as an unexpected gift. Along with the candles came a heartfelt card and such meaningful words written to both Alvin and myself! One candle says "Joy" and the other says "Strength!" Two words, each one significant to the other.

It touched our hearts and made us realize that so many people we love have had a challenging 2021! Some have lost their "joy" and their "strength" through the struggles this year has brought. Some have faced illnesses, loneliness, financial hardships, abuse, divorce, miscarriages, lost dreams, lack of connections with family, being misunderstood, and the list goes on! We too have had to fight battles this past year with the loss of loved ones, numerous and extended hospital visits, and constantly moving goal posts and uncertainties.

Life can seem so unfair at times, and sometimes in the valleys we find many hindrances to seeing the hand of God! In the midst of the sufferings, confusion, and anxiety, we need both joy and strength more than ever!

During tough times, the core of our joy is going to be in our relationship with God and the certainty of His love. The fruit of the Spirit that has been cultivated and growing in our lives is still available in the hard times because of that endless and abundant love. When we stand in the truth and acceptance of His love for us, we can be nourished by that fruit.

> *But the fruit produced by the Holy Spirit within you is* divine love *in all its varied expressions:* joy that overflows, *peace that subdues, patience that endures, kindness in action, a life full of virtue, faith that prevails, gentleness of heart, and strength of spirit . . . they are meant to be limitless."*
> —Galatians 5:22–23a, TPT (emphasis added).

If we look to the Old Testament, we are reminded that it is the joy of the Lord that *is* our strength (Nehemiah 8:10b).

Gratitude plays a big part in helping us to see joy become our strength. Many of us want to cultivate a joyful spirit, but it's not something we can do through our own power. Since joy is a fruit of the Holy Spirit, we must allow the breath of the Spirit to help move us in the direction of joy. This is why we give thanks in the midst of every circumstance, trusting God's love to sustain and strengthen us. Nothing can separate us from His love.

My prayer for you today is that if you've lost your joy or your strength, you will look around and find the small miracles that you've missed noticing. Today may you find things for which to be grateful, even in the everyday pain and frustrations of life that may get in the way. May you find a new joy released and experience your strength renewed.

> *Lord, sometimes my body and mind become tired and weak from searching for reasons to rejoice. I pray for strength, and I invite you to remind me of the fruit of the Spirit available in my life. Give me the perseverance, motivation, and ability to not give up. Quiet my heart in your presence. May your abiding joy and perfect peace find residence in my heart as I rest in your love. I give thanks today for your unfailing goodness. In Jesus' name.*

Embracing Surrender

Day Eleven

Contributed by Christine Dobrocky

Those who sow in tears shall reap in joy.

—Psalm 126:5, NKJV

For many years I was confused about the concept of surrender. I'd convinced myself that I had it all figured out, only to find out that I was completely clueless. It wasn't until I recently entered into a personal relationship with God that I began to understand what a fully surrendered life meant.

Life in the police force brings more than its share of trauma and struggle. When responsibilities must be cared for, many times traumatic, taking the time for needed personal care can often be delayed and resultingly debilitating. A twelve-step recovery program for an eating disorder was a divine intervention to my need for help. It was there that the concept of surrender was introduced to me, and the soil of my heart was cultivated in preparation for God's purposes in the days ahead.

I assumed that if I told others I was ready to surrender my life to God, everything would fall into place. I imagined the joy that I longed for would descend from heaven in the form of a beautiful mourning dove. I discovered, however, that nothing could be further from the truth. Words alone proved to be empty promises that I had no strength to fulfil. It was during a fifteen-month relapse in my recovery that I began to associate the word "surrender" with pain, not joy. The harder I attempted to surrender my life, the more tears I shed. I realize now that I had a life-crippling grip on the main culprit that gets in the way of surrender: control.

Experiencing Joy

It was a sunny summer day, sitting by the water's edge and feeling the power of waves roll over one another, when out of nowhere a tsunami of tears began to gush down my face. In that moment my life was forever changed. I experienced for the first time what I now know was the power of the Holy Spirit. That was when I began to understand what true joy felt like—zero effort or control were a part of the equation that day. I'd been searching for joy in a pleasure-filled, materialistic lifestyle, focused on seeking the approval of others. God provided me with the reassurance that I could surrender everything to Him. He took away the pain associated with the shame and guilt that I'd been carrying for decades. His healing power touched my life. In a matter of twenty-four hours, I went from living in complete despair to feeling the joy that came from trusting God with my entire life. The death grip that control had over my life was released with absolutely no effort. For nearly a month my entire being was bathing in an abundance of God's love and acceptance, and an unexplainable, unfamiliar joy.

Though it's still early in my walk as a Christian woman, I've learned that in order to experience an outflow of love and joy from the Holy Spirit, a surrendered life is an absolute must. The instant I start to feel my joy being pulled out from under my feet, I do the surrender test and ask myself: "Am I in a place of control or surrender?" God knows what's best for me and has shown me that embracing a surrendered life allows me to experience a joy and peace that no amount of money can bring, no friendship can fulfill, and no attention or applause can satisfy.

My hope for others who are walking through pain is that they will trust God as their safe place, their protector and healer, and that they will embrace a surrendered life. As they do, God will make good of their tears and open an internal peace and joy that surpasses all understanding!

Heavenly Father, my desire is to willingly trust you, even in the very challenging seasons. Forgive me for trying to steer my own course independently of you. I hand to you my fears, my disappointments, my failure, and my need to control. Thank you for welcoming my surrender and restoring my joy.

A Father's Joy

Day Twelve

From a long distance away, his father saw him coming… The father raced out to meet him, swept him up in his arms, hugged him dearly, and kissed him over and over with tender love.

—Luke 15:20, TPT

For many months the father's heart had been breaking as he watched the increasing turbulence in the life of his younger son. There had been signs of restlessness, rebellion, and disrespect. The need for independence and immediate gratification had been persistent. Now he was asking for his inheritance. It seemed irrational, especially when the farm was thriving and he lacked nothing, but the father saw no reason to withhold the inheritance from him.

As this parable recorded in Luke goes, the father watched this wild and demanding son as he gathered up his belongings and took off to enjoy life, leaving his big brother behind to run the family business with his father. His impetuous nature and unteachable character made it clear that he didn't have a plan for his future, and he didn't seem to care. This wasn't what the father had planned for this son he loved. He had dreams for him that were grand and glorious.

The throbbing pain in his heart was undeniable. He would wait with patience, investing faith and hope for the anticipated day of his prodigal's return. While he waited, he trusted, his heart reliving the joy of his birth.

Experiencing Joy

Father made many trips to the laneway, likely never missing a day, in faith that today might be the day he would see him again. He would envision the grand reunion, feel the joy, then weep and return to his work.

But on this particular afternoon, the father's dream became a reality. When the son was still a long way down the road, his believing, rejoicing father ran to meet him. *"He swept him up in his arms, hugged him dearly, and kissed him over and over with tender love."* There was no question of his love and forgiveness—it was conspicuous and extravagant. These were actions that expressed a joy that flowed from a love deep within. Perhaps it was the same delight that made David dance and the paralyzed man on the temple stairs go walking and leaping and praising God when he was healed.

There are many lessons to be gleaned from this parable. In an entire lifetime, we're not likely to fully understand just how much God loves and treasures us as His sons and daughters. We can't even faintly fathom the extent of His patience and love extended to us when we choose our own rebellious detours.

Have you ever considered the joy the scripture says is felt in heaven over one sinner that repents? The party is real—the details of the fatted calf, the feast, and the celebration serve to remind us that there is no greater joy for our Heavenly Father than to have us found at home with Him, sharing in His work, attending to Kingdom business, and enjoying His presence. From that place He can teach us, train us, lavish us with His love, and release us into the joy of His purposes and plans for our life. He is truly a good, good Father.

Father, today I look down the laneway of faith once again for those I love but who have chosen a path of their own, far away from your love. I am reminded of the party that awaits their return, their welcome, and your forgiveness. As I wait, I choose to rejoice in the plans and purposes of Heaven over their lives, and I declare that they too will not be able to resist your relentless love!

The Joyful News

Day Thirteen

Then the angel said to [the shepherds], "Do not be afraid, for behold, I bring you good tidings of great joy which will be to all people."
—Luke 2:10, NKJV

It's an obvious understatement to say we live in a day of great fear. Social media misinformation in peak proportions, fearmongering amongst politicians, panic-driven newscasters, wars and rumours of wars—it's challenging to find peace and even daring to expect joy.

Tucked into the rotating attacks on our peace comes the celebration of Christmas. A great sigh of relief followed by some long-needed giggles of delight are always provided by the annual Christmas interviews with the children of our church. Some of my favourite kids' responses to questions about the first Christmas include: "It's special because Jesus was born just in time for Christmas up at the North Pole." "There was sheep, cows, chickens ... mmm, but I liked the reindeer best." "There was Mary and Joseph and a danger." "They brought gifts like Lego and gold and they found toys from Santa under the straw." "The wise men and elves and some really big angels all sang songs 'cause they were so excited." Amid the clutter of our daily cares and fears, the innocence and freshness of a child can be a priceless gift of renewal.

As we draw ourselves into the story, we hear the word of the angel to Mary: "Do not be afraid!" The same word came to Joseph in a dream: "Don't be afraid." And to the shepherds in a field, keeping watch over their flocks by night: *"Do not be afraid, for behold, I bring you good tidings of great joy which will be to all people. For there is born to you this day in the city of David a Savior, who is Christ the Lord"* (Luke 2:10–11, NKJV). There it is, the hope in place of fear—the joyful announcement that a baby would be born who would be the Saviour of the world.

Bret Harte in his classic short story "The Luck of Roaring Camp" tells of the birth of a baby on the American frontier, a baby that made a radical change in a rough-and-tumble mining camp. The only woman in the camp, Cherokee Sal, a disreputable woman at best, died in childbirth, leaving a healthy young baby boy to be raised by the now all-male camp.

These rough, hard men decided they didn't want any more women who weren't nice hanging around their baby—they would raise the child themselves. They prepared a cabin for little "Tommy Luck" and kept it scrupulously clean. The rosewood cradle they purchased for the baby made the rest of the cabin look wretched, so they had to do more fixing up. Anyone who wanted to hold Tommy Luck had to clean up for that privilege.

Each act of cleanliness exposed more of the surrounding dirt, so ongoing measures were initiated to clean up the camp. Since the baby needed rest, the camp became quieter and more dignified, no longer the "Roaring Camp" of the story's title. The story of the baby of Roaring Camp is the story of the regeneration of a group of people. That baby changed the whole atmosphere of the Roaring Camp and brought revelation that changed those within,

And so it was two thousand years ago in Bethlehem. The birth of a baby changed everything. Our good news of great joy was the coming of a newborn child. It was an unpretentious event in the humblest of settings yet our greatest gift of joy. When that gift is received and welcomed into our hearts by faith, we too will experience transformation and peace.

> *Oh Holy Child of Bethlehem, descend to us, we pray; cast out our sin and enter in, be born in us today. We hear the Christmas angels the great glad tidings tell; O come to us, abide with us, our Lord Emmanuel!*[2]

---

2   Phillips Brooks, 1868, https://hymnary.org/text/o_holy_child_of_bethlehem_descend_to_us.

Joyful Praise

Day Fourteen

Contributed by Vanessa Brobbel

Come, let's sing for joy to the Lord, let's shout joyfully to the rock of our salvation.
—Psalm 95:1, NASB

I don't know what carpooling kids in your car looks like, but in ours, there is *always* music. We sing loudly, passionately, and sometimes more than a little off-key! It doesn't take long into a trip before even the most painfully shy passengers start bopping to the music, because joyful praise is contagious! We've journeyed through many challenges, but we've learned that joyful praise can open even the tightly-gripped fists of pain.

Our family has always loved to sing, but there was a turning point when singing turned to praise, and praise turned pain into joyful gratitude. This is a sound bite of that journey ...

Through a series of circumstances, we found ourselves in Calgary, Alberta. My health had tanked, as had the business venture we'd moved there to begin. We knew that God had called us there, yet everything seemed to be going wrong! One morning I cried, "Lord! What gives?"

Then the Lord reminded me that in the game of Scrabble, you must have the difficult letters in your hand to win, because they're worth more points. "Vanessa, I'm handing you the tough letters, because I've called you to overcome and succeed at a master's level. I'm asking you to play the Q."

We tend to think of difficulty and pain as punishment, lack of favour, fault, or failure, but God was teaching me to look past the pain and instead trust that this was an opportunity for us to move strategically across the board. I was learning that God was far more interested in my character than my comfort. This message of *character versus comfort* being burned into us was soon a message for which God began opening doors of opportunity for us to share. The "Q" was being played when it seemed like we had completely missed the mark with no "U" in sight.

Our efforts were overwhelmingly blessed, which led to an unexpected phone call from the leadership at Voice of the Martyrs Canada (VOMC). Would we be willing to move back to Ontario to serve on staff? We had *just* signed a lease agreement for the house we were renting, but my husband, Floyd, promised we would talk it over and pray. Within minutes, the phone rang again. It was our landlord pleading with us to break the rental agreement. He needed to sell. Following His cloud, Floyd headed back to Ontario in a packed U-Haul.

The kids and I followed soon after. The day we pulled onto the Trans-Canada highway, we hit dead-stopped traffic due to construction. People were getting out of their vehicles. We hadn't moved in over an hour. There was no way I could risk letting three small children and a dog loose on the highway, so it was time to turn on the tunes! We began singing every child's praise song known to man, complete with actions. We were laughing and praising God in our cramped little car when *finally* the construction cleared!

Just ahead was that beacon of blessed hope: Tim Horton's! We piled into the restaurant, now filled with frustrated motorists freshly released from the highway. When we walked into their midst, suddenly they began to clap and cheer. Every eye was on ... me? Those angry and irritated travellers had caught sight of a little red Hyundai filled with children and their crazy mother going full steam with "Pharoah, Pharoah! Oh baby, let My people go!" Their frowns became smiles, and that day I learned that *joyful praise is contagious.* Joyful praise born out of pain, submitted to God, has the power to affect more lives than we could ever dream possible!

> *Lord, give me the grace to see that I have a weapon to fight the exasperation and irritation—some joyful praise! Use my praise to change atmospheres as it rises to you. In Jesus' name.*

Morning Is Coming

Day Fifteen

Weeping may endure for a night, but joy comes in the morning.
—Psalm 30:5b, NKJV

Living in a sin riddled world, where humanity regularly faces the struggle of loss, broken relationships, health crises, and other trauma, it would seem we have many reasons to despair. We can feel shattered, wondering if hope will ever return. But God reminds us through the psalmist David that our weeping may endure for a night, but joy will come in the morning.

A night represents a duration—it's the time before the day breaks. It means there's an expiration date for the weeping! We shouldn't panic, however, if the hard place lasts more than twenty-four hours. We need not feel that we have missed God if we're still in emotional or physical pain weeks later. Night here refers to a time frame that I call a season. In Ecclesiastes 3:1, 4, we're assured that *"To everything there is a season, a time for every purpose under heaven . . . A time to weep, and a time to laugh; a time to mourn, and a time to dance"* (NKJV). As painful as a night season may be, it's only a season. Morning will come!

What exactly is morning? Because we are in Jesus Christ, we have His promise that He can take every horrid situation and transform it into something good. He can take the broken places in our lives and create a beautiful mosaic that will bless the world. In Psalm 30:11–12, the psalmist explains that He removes our garments of discomfort and ruin and gives us new garments of joy. Such joy is meant to bring us again into a place of praise.

David was anointed king as a teenager, but he spent many years running and hiding from King Saul. Although those times were difficult, it was during those years that David penned many of the psalms about God's faithfulness and goodness that now comfort millions.

Joseph endured the pit and the prison. That was his night, but joy came in the morning when he was able to embrace his brothers once again.

The Apostle Paul spent two years in a dirty, musty, dark jail cell just for preaching the gospel. Those were night times for him, but they weren't wasted. Joy came in the morning—just check out his letter to the Philippians!

The woman with the issue of blood had a very long night—one that lasted for twelve years and included rejection, physical pain, financial loss, and disappointment. But what a joy when she touched Jesus and her morning came.

We're not talking about the joy of this world, which comes and goes as often as the ocean waves hit the shore. We're talking about something you can cling to for the long haul. For the believer, the fruit of the Spirit, including joy, is like a bottomless well of water—though you may need to go deep to find it, there's always an ample supply.

Consider this: when the night comes, we can't see the sun, but it still exists. It's still there, though out of view. This is like joy. We can trust His promise that morning is coming. Joy is still there ... it's just momentarily out of view. Be encouraged, for joy is sure to break forth, as morning is coming—you can depend on it. Why not begin to declare this truth over your situation today? Allow yourself to envision the sunrise by faith and start allowing His joy to be your strength right now. And as you wait, do so in hope, trusting Him. The triumph of morning is surely on its way.

Father, today I'm deciding to live with a joyful expectation that morning is coming in my circumstances and struggles. Your promises never fail, and I can rest assured that you have a plan and a purpose. I surrender my need to know why and lean into the embrace of your love.

In His Presence

Day Sixteen

Contributed by Stephen Wesley

You reveal the path of life to me; in Your presence is abundant joy; in Your right hand are eternal pleasures.

—Psalm 16:11, HCSB

King David presents here a picture of a wellspring of joy. He identifies joy with a person and strongly assents to the truth that joy is a by-product of a personal relationship with the God of the universe. He tells us that joy comes from the personal presence of this Almighty personhood. David claims that when you are in the presence of this individual, there is abundant joy.

The Hebrew word for "abundant" is *soba*, which means "satiety, i.e., one's fill of food to contentment, all one wants, contentment. Formally, state of contentment and satisfaction, implying abundance."[3] Another way of saying this is that His joy totally satisfies. This joy is like no other joy in circumstances that may be favourable or horrible. His presence changes everything and brings about joy when it would seem to be impossible.

Joy is the word *simha*, meaning "joy, gladness, delight, i.e., a feeling or attitude of joyful happiness and cheerfulness; this is a response to, or manifestation of, worship to God and so transcendent even of unfavorable circumstances; pleasure."[4] God's joy is tangible; it marks you and me as the people of God, for it can be appropriated at all times and in any circumstance because of the presence of the Holy Spirit within.

---

3 James Swanson, *Dictionary of Biblical Languages with Semantic Domains: Hebrew (Old Testament)*, (Oak Harbor: Logos Research Systems, Inc., 1997).

4 Ibid.

Experiencing Joy

I lost my father at a very early age. He passed away when he was thirty-seven. The devastation I felt was earth shattering. Only the compassionate grace of God on my life, even though I didn't know it at the time, carried me through. It was an event that marked my mother as well, turning her back to her childhood faith. She began to run after the Lord with every breath she breathed. At eighty, she was diagnosed with lung cancer. We went to prayer, hopeful and expectant for healing. Such was not the case, and it was a whirlwind of emotion and disappointment. The loss gripped me with a sudden stranglehold. My family asked me to officiate at mother's funeral, and in my weakness, He gave me strength. His grace, once again, carried me through her death and burial.

The next day, however, I found myself in a very dark place and unable to pray. I was in my room of prayer, trying to pray, but no words came. I knew I wasn't abandoned and that this loss was a part of life. My faith had all the answers, but none of the stability and fortitude that it should have brought were present. As the darkness grew, an inner voice asked, "What do you believe?" As the words hit my ears, a fire of faith erupted inside of me. I began to declare the truths of God's Word that I'd built my life upon. It poured out of me like a deluge of rain, and with it the presence of the Lord filled my heart and the entire room. God was in that room, and with His presence came His abundant joy and absolute fortitude of mind. I experienced what David meant in this psalm as I welcomed His presence into my circumstance.

Joy is a person, not just a by-product of ease of life. God's presence is filled with His joy, which transcends life's problems. It's a promise of the eternal pleasures awaiting us when, with unfiltered sight, we behold Him. Be encouraged. You don't have to wait; more joy is available right now, in His presence.

Jesus, there is no one like you. In your presence is abundant joy. Help me to cultivate Your presence in my life. Silence the distractions that keep me from your presence and set me on fire for you.

Joy Trumps Them All

Day Seventeen
Contributed by John Courtney

Rejoice in the Lord always. I will say it again: Rejoice!

—Philippians 4:4

Joy has relatives—Laughter and Happiness are both cousins. While they're related to Joy and are often seen together, they're not the same.

My life has had a dominant flavour of laughter. I have no idea how it came to be, but when I'm with others, I love making and seeing people laugh in a good way—and frequently at my expense. It's not included in the list of spiritual gifts, but the Bible does affirm its value. Laughter isn't appropriate in all situations, but it can bring a welcomed refreshment to what often can be a pretty intense world we live in. I have a special place in my heart for playing the game Rook, especially with my siblings. The longer the game goes on, the more one of us will need to ask, "What's trump?"—meaning which of these identified cards holds the greatest strength or power over the others in a particular game? You can't win the game without this information. Laughter is powerfully present in the banter. And as much as this refreshes my spirit, "Joy trumps Laughter." Laughter is a second cousin to joy.

Happiness is a first cousin to Joy. It's a higher quality relationship than second cousin Laughter. It's more of a state of mind and heart than an emotional expression. While both are often accompanied by a smile, Happiness is richer, of higher quality.

Life moves through seasons—some change rather quickly. Sometimes Happiness leaves the room when unexpected events and circumstances open a door to deep sorrow or disappointment. When Happiness is present, it's a beautiful gift, a treasure. I've experienced this in abundance, but "Joy trumps Happiness."

So what is joy? Paul exhorts us in Philippians 4:4 to *"Rejoice in the Lord always. I will say it again: Rejoice!"* It sounds like joy is something to which we're called. It's a fruit of the Spirit as listed in Galatians 5:22, which means it's true source for us as Christ followers is the Holy Spirit. Matthew suggests that joy can be present in the midst of life's most difficult circumstances (5:11). He connects joy to our belief that we have an eternity in heaven.

Jesus had a very interesting conversation about this with his seventy-two sent-out followers in Luke 10. They came back so happy—filled with joy because they had experienced God at work with all kinds of miracles. And so they should be. Maybe they were all high-fiving each other. But Jesus calls them to a proper focus. He says to them *"... do not rejoice that the spirits submit to you, but rejoice that your names are written in heaven"* (Luke 10:20)—a great reminder that our joy must be connected to our focus on eternity ... heaven.

Joy is not so much a feeling as it is a focus. In Hebrews 12, the writer attributes his commitment to living out his life in obedience to Jesus to a focus on what lies ahead. He reminds us that this is what Jesus did as well, since the joy set before Him gave Him strength to endure the cross. This brings us back to the source of joy. Even Luke suggests that Jesus' joy was from the Holy Spirit: *"Jesus, full of joy through the Holy Spirit"* (Luke 10:21). Joy is a fruit of the Spirit working in our lives.

So how do we embrace joy? We do our best to push away all the noise and find a place of solitude and quietness. Then we allow the Holy Spirit to reveal God's incredible love for us and His plans for us to be with Him forever in eternity. We draw near and choose to be with Him, the One who is waiting for us. There we find joy.

Jesus, I'm choosing to draw near to you today, to embrace joy, to abide and allow you to reveal again your incredible love. In the quiet place with you, I am in awe.

Joy Challenged

Day Eighteen
Contributed by Ed and Lori McKay

Do not forget to rejoice, for hope is always just around the corner. Hold up through the hard times . . . and devote yourselves to prayer.
—Romans 12:12, VOICE

We heard his story of shelters, foster homes, a prior adoption breakdown, and then back into foster care. Now, at age seven, they were looking for new adoptive parents for this bright young boy, D. They preferred more experienced parents, but we sold ourselves to the overseeing agency—to adopt this boy we'd never even met. A difficult part was that there was to be *no* talk of adoption for two whole years, giving him time to heal and making sure we could manage together. What would we have to "manage," and why were they hesitant?

"Well, D, how do you like the meals at your new foster home?" the CAS worker asked.

D promptly replied, "Ed is a good cook, and Lori gives it a good effort!" The room erupted with laughter as D made the rounds from adult to adult. His trust with strangers was disturbing—attachment issues were evident.

Even with the child psychiatrist's diagnoses and prescribed medications in place, we found that life was very difficult for D, with almost daily meltdowns. Still, we were desperately trying to bond with this dear boy. Therapists, pastor friends, social workers, and a loving church family all supported us, but it was a roller coaster of emotions—from the pit of perceived failure to the short-lived moments of success.

Experiencing Joy

Joy? It really seemed more important just staying afloat! If anything, it was mainly the joy that scripture commands. That joy is an action that can be engaged in regardless of feelings or circumstances—the joy that's possible only as a fruit of the Holy Spirit in our lives. As James said, count it as joy as testing works endurance, maturity, and hope (James 1:2).

We received an offer to pastor a church in northern Ontario and were given permission to take D with us. Just after his tenth birthday, we celebrated his adoption! Our dreams of his adoption and of pastoring had both fallen into place. Did that signing of papers move life into a satisfying rhythm of good reports? We wish! As a family, we processed together, implementing the most workable strategies. We believed together for God's healing, and we lived out forgiveness daily. Still, we were less than the ideal happy Christian family we had imagined.

Finally, at age eleven, with a more accurate diagnosis, we had a greater understanding of D's struggles and how to support him, but healthy attachment concerns remained. We celebrated every small victory and found joy in simple successes. We discovered home-schooling worked best for D for the next three years, and by junior high, he was able to function half days in school. He flourished without incident in high school and continued on to university, acing a difficult math program and, at the same time, receiving a minor in computer science.

Following graduation, D began full-time employment and is now thriving at his job. He continues to grow in a quiet but sincere faith in God. He met a beautiful young lady at his church, and they dated for five years. Having just passed their second wedding anniversary, we thank God for D's honouring, his generosity, and his affectionate care toward his wife.

We cried, prayed, and worshipped our way through the years of struggles and back into the joy of recognizing that our caring heavenly Father had been always cheering us on. We had our eye on a goal that only a miracle of His love and grace could accomplish. We know now the wisdom of Paul's instruction: *"Do not forget to rejoice, for hope is always just around the corner."* We serve a great God.

Jesus, you truly are a way-maker. In those times when I feel weak and overwhelmed, help me to trust. Where I feel defeated, may the strength of your joy bring me fresh perseverance and hope.

Knowing His Voice

Day Nineteen
Contributed by Chidi Opara

You have not seen him, but you love him ... and so you rejoice with an indescribable and glorious joy.
—1 Peter 1:8b, NET

In the book of Acts, we read of Peter's deliverance from jail. An angel came while he slept and led him secretly past four squads of soldiers placed by Herod to keep guard. The angel then walked with him through a city gate that opened by itself. After seeing Peter safely away from the prison, he disappeared.

Peter could hardly believe what had just happened, but he headed straight to the home of Mary, the mother of John Mark, where many were in deep payer for his release.

When he knocked at the door of the gate, a slave woman named Rhoda came to answer. When she recognized Peter's voice, because of her joy she did not open the gate, but ran in and announced that Peter was standing in front of the gate. They said to her, "You are out of your mind!" But she kept insisting that it was so ... Peter continued knocking ...
—Acts 12:13–16a, NASB

Rhoda was a maid at Mary's house and knew why the believers were praying at that time. It was public news that James had been killed and Peter was next. Only a miracle would save him now. Peter must have been a regular visitor to this location because Rhoda knew his voice distinctly—she could identify Peter's voice without opening the gate to see him.

Experiencing Joy

Joy can do that sometimes—interrupt even the mundane task of opening a gate. While Rhoda, as a maid, was in no place to argue with the unbelieving disciples, she kept insisting that Peter was at the door! Even after being ridiculed and accused of being out of her mind, she persisted. Her knowledge of the *voice of Peter* gave her a confident joy to stand by her claim.

Our joy is often fully expressed in the presence of God (Psalm 16:11). His joy can withstand ridicule and even heartbreak. For us, a steadfast joy can be found in hearing the *voice of the Lord*. Recognizing and obeying His voice is essential for every believer to function effectively. When God speaks to me, I know something is about to change for good.

In 2020, my wife lost her father, and the news was devastating. Watching her cry intensely, unable to lessen her pain, frustrated me. I asked the Lord, "What do I do now? Please, Lord, just say something." After a few minutes, I heard God say, "Worship," and I knew when I heard His voice that a solution was on its way. I picked up my guitar and started worshipping next to my wife. I thought she was going to be really upset with me, perhaps feeling I wasn't sensitive her sadness. But instead of listening to the voice of ridicule and worry in my head, I kept worshipping. To my surprise, after one hour of worship, she joined me, and we worshipped for another hour. Together we gave Him not only the pain and deep sense of loss, but our gratitude, and the joy of the Lord became her strength (Nehemiah 8:10). When we lean into the voice of the Lord, that voice can release in us an exceeding joy, one that brings comfort, assurance, peace, and refreshing.

If the voice of Peter could generate that much excitement in Rhoda at God's answer to their prayer, how much more joy we must have at *the voice of the Lord God Himself.* Today I pray that God would grant you a confident joy that comes from recognizing His voice and yielding to His call.

Jesus, though not always seeing you in my situations, I confess that I do believe. Let the sound of your voice release in me the joy and peace that flows from the assurance that you are right here.

Hannah's Joy

Day Twenty

Then Hannah prayed and said, "My heart rejoices in the Lord; my horn is exalted in the Lord... I rejoice in Your salvation. There is no one holy like the Lord, indeed, there is no one besides You, nor is there any rock like our God."
—1 Samuel 2:1–2, NASB

There is no better way for children to get a head start in life than to have a godly mother. Jochebed birthed Moses; Elizabeth birthed John the Baptist. Behind Timothy was his mother, Eunice, and behind Samuel was the godly and grateful Hannah.

Hannah's barrenness was not only a matter of regret, but a reproach. She was a woman of sorrowful spirit. Her long-time infertility had confined her to a place of social embarrassment and loneliness. On top of that, she shared her husband, Elkanah, with Peninnah, a woman of ample fertility who ridiculed her with jeers and hurtful words. Hannah's story, recorded in 1 Samuel 1 and 2, is one of fortitude and faith in the midst of pain and mockery, but it's also a story of a fulfilled promise of God that brought great rejoicing.

Year after year as they went up to the house of the Lord to bring their sacrifice, Peninnah would provoke Hannah about her infertility. On one particular visit, Hannah's emotions erupted into tears. She wept until she couldn't even eat. She confessed to Eli, the priest, that she was actually pouring out her soul to the Lord, recognizing afresh that her relief was in God alone. She was pleading with God to give her a son. She vowed that if God answered her prayer, she would give the child to Him to be His servant in the temple. Eli prophesied to her, *"Go in peace; and may the God of Israel grant your request that you have asked of him*" (I Samuel 1:17, NASB). Her response to God's promise was worship. She left, believing in His power to do great things.

Within hours, her infertility was ended, and Samuel was conceived. Hannah raised Samuel until he was ready to be weaned, and then she prepared to bring him to the Tabernacle of the Lord in Shiloh to fulfill the promise she'd made to God. Her prayer had been answered, and she didn't forget about the One who had answered it. Samuel was released to live under Eli's supervision and minister at the Tabernacle all the days of his life.

The true heart and character of this noble woman is revealed in "Hannah's Prayer" in I Samuel 2:1–11. Hannah lifts her voice in a song of joy expressing God's victory, not only for herself but for the whole nation of Israel, for all the people of God. What courage! She sings a song of praise and gratitude, one of God's sovereign redemption. God has delivered Hannah from her disgrace to a position of honour and strength.

Hannah was an extraordinary woman of integrity and faith. It's no wonder Samuel became such a great prophet. Hannah was a model mother. She understood pain and how to keep praying. She hid nothing from God, and she continued to worship as she awaited Heaven's response. She trusted God to fulfill His promise, and she kept her vow at tremendous personal cost.

What was the secret to Hannah's strength? How could she have had joy as she handed over her only child to be raised by someone else for the rest of his life? The answer is profound. The supreme source of Hannah's joy was not in the child but in the God who had answered her prayer. Although Hannah cherished Samuel with her whole heart, the gift was not greater than the Giver. When we learn to rejoice in the Lord Himself and not merely in His blessings, we too can expect to experience such joy.

Heavenly Father, I haven't always seen you as greater than the gifts and blessings. I ask your forgiveness and trust your guidance to help me set the right priorities. May my songs of victory always celebrate who you are—you are a good, good Father.

Liberating Joy

Day Twenty-One

Your laws are my joyous treasure forever.

—Psalm 119:111, TLB

Hezekiah was the twelfth king of Judah, who began his rule in 726 BC. As a king, he was dedicated to God and to the spiritual progress of the nation. While his father, Ahaz, closed the temple and abandoned its services (2 Chronicles 28:24), Hezekiah's first move was to purge, repair, and reopen the temple. He sent letters throughout Judah and Israel urging everyone to return to God, to realign themselves with God's covenant. He reminded them of the need for submission and obedience to God's commands, especially the Passover.

The Passover celebration commemorated the time when God had spared the lives of Israel's firstborn sons in Egypt. He had sent a plague to kill the firstborn sons in the land unless the blood of a slain lamb had been applied to the door posts. The Israelites obeyed, and God passed over those houses, doing no harm. After that plague, Pharaoh freed the Israelites from slavery. The Passover was an annual celebration when they were to remember how God had delivered his people.

In 2 Chronicles 30, we read about this particular Passover invitation from Hezekiah and observe how obedience to God's laws resulted in great joy. Obedience to laws sounds rather restrictive and heavy, but here we identify a strange and unconventional pairing—a liberating joy that lies in choosing obedience to God's laws.

For those who had accepted the invitation to celebrate the Passover week together, the hand of God was on them to walk in unity in what the king commanded (v. 12). The people consecrated themselves to prepare for worship, and the mood of the celebration was one of great joy. In fact, the joy was of such intensity that the people decided to extend the celebration an extra week! For an additional seven days they celebrated joyfully. Since the days of Solomon, there had been nothing like this. That was a two-hundred-year joy deficit! What Hezekiah did was not just a brilliant idea. He was acting to obey the laws of God commanded through Moses for the people of Israel. It was part of his effort to return the people to God's laws as a standard for living.

In Matthew 5:17–19, Jesus says that He hasn't come to abolish the law but to fulfil it. The laws find their fullest meaning in Jesus. His life clarifies and communicates God's will for us, and His life of perfect obedience to the will of God made Him the perfect sacrifice for sin. As we grow in Him, the Spirit of God produces in us the fruit of the Spirit, including joy. The life of Jesus models the principles and commands meant to guide our lives.

Choosing to heed His commands to repent, to follow Him, to let our light shine before others, to forgive, to love our enemies, to pray for one another, to refrain from judging others, to seek first the Kingdom of God are all meant to help us experience His joy. *"If you keep my commandments, you will abide in my love, just as I have kept my Father's commandments and abide in his love. These things I have spoken to you, that my joy may be in you, and that your joy may be full"* (John 15:10–11, ESV). Obedience to His commands will unearth a magnificent treasure of *liberating joy* that only He can provide.

Heavenly Father, I want to be one of those who follows your commands and lives a life that brings pleasure and honour to your name. It's my way of truly showing you how much I love you. I know that obedience will release your promises of abundant blessings of joy over my life. I receive today's reminder from your Word to align my steps once again with yours so that I might see the fulfilment of every plan and purpose you have for my life. In Jesus' name. Amen.

Ridiculous Joy

Day Twenty-Two
Contributed by Lori Webster

The steps of the God-pursuing ones follow firmly in the footsteps of the Lord, and God delights in every step they take to follow him.

—Psalm 37:23, TPT

I could tell my brother was excited when he visited that summer. The reason for that excitement? He had a new and challenging job opportunity for me! He had my attention—but the job was in South Korea! Was he serious? I had my future desires well-strategized and clearly expressed to God. Stay in Niagara, get married, have a family. Done! Going to South Korea would derail my intentions, and at thirty-four there wasn't a lot of wiggle room.

I was invited to the home of my coworker's parents in Haliburton for the weekend and shared this out-of-the-box notion with them. For me, it had created a dilemma of both curiosity and concern. Her mom promptly but thoughtfully offered her spiritual assessment: "I see this for you like the Macedonian call." Following a time of prayer with some other friends who had joined us, a second word was expressed: "You're going to be making a decision sooner than you think!" My thoughts raced, my heart began to call out for help, and some serious prayer for direction got underway.

Sure enough, the next day, back to work in my very secure and fulfilling ministry job, an email arrived from my brother's contact, Pastor Hannah, in South Korea. It was an invitation to come and teach at their English Academy. To my utter amazement, the letter closed with a verse from Acts 16:9: "*Come over to Macedonia and help us.*" I was instantly in tears, and as I shared the reason with my co-workers, they expressed a joy and enthusiasm for me over the possibility.

Over the next few weeks, God began to make it clear that this was His set-up. While I vacillated, He was patient. When I struggled to find peace, He quieted my heart. When that memorable phone call came from South Korea, I listened intently to Pastor Hannah's words, and they settled like a welcomed spring rain. She and the children really felt I was supposed to be their teacher. The conflict ceased, and I said yes right away. Perhaps I was more afraid than excited, but I was thanking God for not letting me miss what was clearly His path for me.

Arrangements were made to get a visa, and I prepared to tie things up at my job. One day as I was leaving my workplace here at home (located next to an elementary school), a bubbly, bright-eyed little girl came skipping toward me. "Are you my new teacher?" she asked. Though I was certainly not her new teacher, I knew God had arranged this moment to let me know there were children in South Korea waiting for me! I tasted Heaven's joy. It was a magnificent opportunity that He had orchestrated.

Many miles and another hemisphere later, I was walking along the river in the sunshine, in a picturesque spot in South Korea. I was feeling such *ridiculous joy*—that's the only way it can be described! Why should I, walking alone in a foreign country, further away than ever from my own dreams being fulfilled, be grinning away and exploding with joy? I realized that true joy might not be found when your dreams come true but in your obedience to a good God, whose plans are greater and whose thoughts are higher than you had imagined.

Father God, sometimes your plans are so very different from the ones I have in mind. Help me to trust you, knowing that as we take each next step together, your fullness of joy will follow.

The King's Delight

Day Twenty-Three

The Lord your God is with you, the Mighty Warrior who saves. He will take great delight in you; in his love he ... will rejoice over you with singing.
—Zephaniah 3:17

These words in Zephaniah 3:17 were primarily addressed to Israel, the chosen people. They foreshadow the blessings of justice, purification, gladness, and restoration that are yet to be realized. But the wider circle, all of us who have been grafted in, may appropriate their blessing. The King of Israel is in the midst of his people. The Holy One who inhabits eternity has taken up residence in those who belong to Him. Is there anything more wonderful? God, our mighty warrior who saves us, is daily taking great delight in us. I can't think of anything that should motivate us more to be like Jesus.

Can you sense the tenderness of this joy? It's a joy springing out of love, the joy of one who seeks the happiness of another. In that joy there is no element of selfishness. It is pure affection. It is intense, deep, breaking into song. To know and love this Creator who rejoices over us is to find purpose and meaning in life: "*We love Him because He first loved us*" (1 John 4:19, NKJV). Ours is a joy of gratitude for the free and full salvation he has given through Jesus Christ. The joy of being delivered from a power who threatened us with utter destruction. The joy of a redeemed one. The joy of His infinite goodness.

I was blessed to spend an exceptional amount of time with my Grandma Dinnick when I was growing up. She was a woman of faith and endless encouragement. She made room for everyone, always looking to bless—the person on the street, her neighbours, the owner of the largest town business, the multiple pastors and leaders of churches in the community. She represented the attitude of Heaven and the delight of God to each of them in unique ways.

I was no less of a recipient of her delight. When I was away working at summer camps in my teen years, she'd write me letters, reminding me that I had the ability to do anything if I tried. She believed in me and she encouraged me. She made me believe it would be hard to fail. She reminded me that God's love would see me through. When I went off to teachers' college, she wrote to me regularly with reminders of my commitment to Christ and my certain success. Her joy leapt off the pages.

When I was home, it was no different. She wouldn't allow me to waver in challenges but reminded me of what she knew to be true. She'd be on the edge of her seat (and very likely on her knees) until I returned with a favourable report. I knew she was with me, cheering me on. She took great delight in me. Her love for me often saved me from the rebuke I probably deserved. Every detail of success and Kingdom fulfilment in my life brought her joy. If there were no recent victories to report, she was simply delighted that we were together.

If in our humanity we're blessed to taste of such love and delight, it serves only to remind us of the incredible truth that the King of kings takes delight in us, singing over us with joy. Pause for a moment right now ... sense His pleasure. You'll gain a fresh desire to draw near and walk in obedience. And as you do, lean your ear Heavenward, in awe, and you just may hear a chord of that beautiful melody He's singing over you.

O Lord, I so seldom take time just to feel your pleasure in me. I feel so undeserving and unworthy of your attention. But wow—you take great delight in me, even singing over me. Teach me to listen for your melodies of love that will draw me closer, and help me to understand your heart in a greater way.

The Joy of Protection

Day Twenty-Four

Contributed by Ryan Harmon

> But let all who take refuge in you rejoice; let them ever sing for joy, and spread your protection over them, that those who love your name may exult in you.
> —Psalm 5:11, ESV

Last week as I organized the tools in my garage, I found myself humming a familiar tune: "I've got the joy (joy, joy, joy) down in my heart (where?), down in my heart ..." The song would start and stop with every interruption from my four-year-old. "Dad, what does this do?" he would ask, picking up a screwdriver from my bag. "What's this for, Dad?" Since becoming a father, I've realized that very little of what I've come to know as "common-sense" exists within humans during the early years. Moses continued sorting through my bag. "Wow, what's this?" he exclaimed as he reached for my saw, ready to grab it by the blade. I acted quickly, interrupting his reach and grabbing his hand just before his tiny fingers met the power-tool. "*Ouch!*" he shrieked.

It's funny how quickly you can experience a gamut of emotions in such a short amount of time with a child. In no more than two minutes, I went from a relaxed state, grateful for the spring sun as it graced my son and me through our garage window, to consoling my son as he sat on my knee clutching his hand, tears sliding down his round cheeks like penguins off an iceberg. I wrapped my arms around his tiny frame, kissed his dirty-blond head, and continued to make melody to myself: *down in my heart (where?), down in my heart ... I've got joy ...* Oh, the irony.

But was it really *that* ironic? Over the last few years, I've come to realize that joy isn't so much a *mood* as it is a state of *being*. Think about it. If your mood—the emotional place that you find yourself in at any given moment—is the gatekeeper of joy in your life, you and I are both in for a rough journey ahead. Between wars, political upheaval, social media platforms with polarizing debates, national protests, cataclysmic natural disasters, etc., we're straight out of luck when it comes to staying eternally chipper.

Joy is a lot like the anchor tied to a boat in a storm. Though the waves beat against the boat, and the wind pushes from every direction, the anchor holds position and doesn't allow the boat to go very far. In Christ, we have an unlimited source of joy available in every season. We have joy in a secure salvation and in sins forgiven. We have joy in knowing that He counsels us through His Word and by His Spirit. We have joy in knowing that He has great plans for our success.

We can even experience joy in following His commands. The devil wants you to believe that God's boundaries—His rules and statues—are barriers between you and an amazing new life. This couldn't be further from the truth! Just like recognizing that love sets some safety guidelines for my son, God's commandments are our protection so that we fully grasp the love He has for us.

My son's tears didn't bring a smile to my face, and truthfully, I hate to see him cry. However, knowing the alternative of what could have happened, I rejoiced knowing that he wasn't harmed. Though rules can often feel like roadblocks, they're put in place for our protection and preservation … a truth that leads me to a question.

What would happen if you chose to change the way you view God's boundaries? If you chose to change your perspective of seeing God as the inhibitor of your fun to welcoming Him as the protector of what He loves? You could have joy infuse your situation right this moment!

Jesus, I realize that your hand reaches down, out of love, for my protection. I rejoice in the plans you have for me. You are not holding me back but are keeping me deeply anchored in your joy.

A Joy-Filled Knowing

Day Twenty-Five
Contributed by Laura Woodley Osman

How lovely are Your dwelling places, O Lord of hosts! ... My heart and my flesh sing for joy to the living God.

—Psalm 84:1, 2b, AMP

The treasure of my life is knowing God and loving Him. Worship is a celebration of how I have come to know God through Christ, and it's an offering of praise acknowledging the multifaceted splendour of a holy loving and living God. I love John 17:3: *"Now this is eternal life: that they know you, the only true God, and Jesus Christ, whom you have sent."* I'm often drawn to this scripture when meditating on the joy of worship.

My favourite part of worship is the "knowing." There's nothing more precious than His presence. When I'm in worship, I realize there are unlimited reasons to praise God for all I know of Him, yet immeasurable ways to know Him remain undiscovered.

Psalm 16:11 says, *"You make known to me the path of life; you will fill me with joy in your presence, with eternal pleasures at your right hand."* The presence of God is the source of all joy. The more I know Him, the more my heart longs for His presence. The more I worship, the more my joy capacity increases.

It's often said that worship should be a lifestyle. Over time I've attempted to grow in the awareness of God's presence wherever I am and in whatever I'm doing. When I'm successful, I find that every task, emotion, or need is soothed and met with the comfort that I am not alone. It's in these times that I often have some of my sweetest worship moments.

Experiencing Joy

There's an exchange of "knowing" between God and me in the everyday experiences where I turn my heart toward Him, engage with His Holy Spirit, and submit to His lead. As I draw near to Him, He draws near to me (James 4:8). There I find the purest joy in the revelation that the Creator of the universe knows me, loves me, and dwells in me by His Spirit. For that reason alone, I cannot help but rejoice!

Worship has led me into joy, even in very challenging times. My father graduated to heaven when I was twenty-six. He was an incredible man of God whom I will always miss. In the initial stages of grief, worship became a tremendous place of healing and hope for me. From my time in worship, a song was birthed about eternal life. I thought of my dad, forever in God's presence. The words to the chorus say this: "You are alive in invisible realms, joining with those who gather to worship the Lamb. Eternal life for all who believe in Jesus Messiah the great King of kings." When I sing this song, I feel joy about my dad's place in heaven. As much as I feel tremendous loss because of his absence, I also feel increasing hope that I will see him again. Singing of God's Kingdom brings fresh perspective about how temporary our difficulties are.

Whether in vibrant corporate praise or quiet personal devotion, there is much joy in *knowing God* and *being known* as we truly are. It's in that place of connection, paid for by Jesus' precious blood, that all loneliness disappears and I experience a prelude to heaven. He is Emmanuel—God with us. We don't have to wait for heaven to experience His joy. In knowing Him, we can be with Him now, right here in our daily journeys.

Heavenly Father, I pray for an increased awareness of your holy presence. My soul longs for your courts. As I worship, may I learn to partake of all the joy and pleasures found in knowing you.

The Joy of Generosity

Day Twenty-Six

> *The generous man [is a source of blessing and] shall be prosperous and enriched, and he who waters will himself be watered [reaping the generosity he has sown].*
> —Proverbs 11:25, AMP

Generosity has sometimes gotten a bad rap. While it's been labeled a duty, an obligation, an unpleasant requirement for the Christian believer, I see it more as an adventure, a release of gratitude, a step of faith, and definitely a joy. It's that joy that's at the very heart of the gospel.

A generous lifestyle begins with the recognition of who God is. There are principles in God's kingdom that help us understand the value and joy of living a lifestyle of generosity. We know that God is generous. He's generous in forgiveness and grace. He created this earth and gave charge of it to us. He gave His only Son to die a cruel death on the cross to reconcile sinful man unto Himself— that's the ultimate in generosity. His nature is simply generous.

True joy lies in the act of giving without an expectation of receiving something in return. When the generous nature of God is modeled for us, it often becomes a standard by which we learn to live ourselves. I've been blessed to have such modeling. I learned early on that giving had little to do with means and almost everything to do with attitude. I saw it in:

- My grandmother, who saw the blessings in her pantry and fridge as belonging to the neighbourhood as much as to her.
- My mother, who made sure, with great delight, that every missionary family across the globe connected to our broader

church fellowship received a card on their birthday—even when she had to save up to pay for the stamps.
- The amazing church family who always made sure there was something under the Christmas tree for us as kids.
- My father, who sacrificed his pride and comfort to work at an outdoor job in bitter cold for a lengthy season so he could see the joy of a paycheque to feed his family
- My brother Joe, who loves to see a restaurant server cry as he slides them a $50 tip on a $5.00 coffee and toast. It's hard to tell who is happier.
- My husband, who has cheerfully filled my gas tank for over fifty years without being asked. He says it's his "joy."

Together, these and *many* more examples have reminded me to hold loosely to what is in my hands and give it freely and joyfully as God directs, storing up treasure for eternity. Giving opens doors that you didn't know existed. God loves cheerful givers. He wants us to be generous in our time that we give to Him and to others, in our finances that we invest to bless and bring relief to others, in our words of affirmation, and in our material goods, love, and forgiveness. The list is limitless. Generosity is love in action. God so loved the world that He gave. Everything we have is a gift from Him, and our giving is an act of worship to Him (2 Corinthians 9:13).

Would you like God to use you to express His generous love to others? Ask God to grow you in this adventure of giving in new ways today that will fill you with the joy that is truly at the heart of the gospel.

Jesus, I'm inviting you to grow me in generosity in new ways. Remind me to activate my faith even when it involves a sacrifice so that I may participate in this amazing joy.

Jumping for Joy!

Day Twenty-Seven
Contributed by Melissa Bone

Why, as soon as your greeting reached my ears, the child within me jumped for joy!
—Luke 1:44, Phillips

Did you know that babies in the womb jump for joy? I've seen it with my own two doula's eyes and felt the kicks of delight with my two doula's hands.[5] Fetuses have all of their senses already working before birth. They can feel, touch, hear, see, and even taste and smell. It's remarkable and underlines the importance of being loved and nurtured before birth. Knowing this, I've taken the opportunity to bless many babies in utero by doing what I call Christian pregnancy blessings, verbally blessing the baby's identity and destiny. Babies love it! Without a doubt, each time I do this, the baby wiggles vigorously within the mother. They literally jump for joy!

I've taken my cue from the biblical story of a baby who leapt for joy. Baby-to-be John the Baptist did a cartwheel of pure delight—he had good reason to do so! The passage in which this event is recorded is often referred to as "The Visitation." This sounds pretty formal for what was a happy reunion of two pregnant relatives. Mary, the mother of Jesus, was newly pregnant by the Holy Spirit and had to find a safe place where she would be understood, accepted, and encouraged. What better person to run to than her older relative, Elizabeth, the priest's wife, who was also pregnant? Elizabeth was her mentor, confidant, and the first person named in the Bible to have recognized Jesus as her Lord, even before His birth! Let's review the story together:

---

5 A doula is a birth coach for women in labour and delivery.

Experiencing Joy

With little delay Mary got ready and hurried off to the hillside town in Judea where Zacharias and Elisabeth lived. She went into their house and greeted her cousin. When Elisabeth heard her greeting, the unborn child stirred inside her and she herself was filled with the Holy Spirit, and cried out, "Blessed are you among women, and blessed is your child! What an honour it is to have the mother of my Lord come to see me! Why, as soon as your greeting reached my ears, the child within me jumped for joy . . ."

—Luke 1:39–44, Phillips

This passage is unique and astounding in so many ways. Two women, both of whom were with child through miraculous intervention, were meeting together, and the Holy Spirit was in on the visit (even though He hadn't been poured out yet at Pentecost). He filled not only Mama Elizabeth but her baby, John, as well! She instantly prophesied a much-needed blessing upon Mary. Elizabeth left nothing to curiosity—she blessed Mary's identity, she blessed her baby, and then she spoke about her Saviour, her Lord, before He was even visible! Her own baby knew he was in the presence of the Son of God too. He was so excited, he couldn't contain it. In a way, he "spoke" through his actions as his mother spoke through her words. Elizabeth blessed Mary's faith and confirmed her destiny as the mother of Jesus Christ, the Saviour of the world. This blessing ignited Mary's spirit to expresses her own song of gratitude and joy to the Lord.

Joy is tangible. It is felt. Its presence can be seen. It is shareable and transferrable. Consider today allowing the Holy Spirit to use you to bless others with your words and actions, no matter how young or old, and see others jump for joy as well!

Heavenly Father, help me to share the joy that has been cultivated in my life so that others may be blessed and inspired with a renewed hope and vision that will lead them to jump for joy.

Joy in Suffering?

Day Twenty-Eight

Be joyful in hope, patient in affliction, faithful in prayer.

—Romans 12:12

Paul and Silas certainly had reason to be concerned. They were outsiders who had come into the city of Philippi and crossed paths with some wealthy business owners who had quite a unique and substantial source of income—a young girl who, through an evil spirit, could interpret signs and tell fortunes. Paul had commanded a demon to come out of the girl, and once healed, she no longer had her fortune-telling abilities, causing the business owners' money source to dry up. They dragged Paul and Silas to the town magistrates, reporting that they were practising customs unlawful to the Romans. Even the crowd joined in the attack.

Arrested, stripped, severely beaten, flogged, and thrown into the inner cell of the jail in stocks and chains, they were forced to await an uncertain verdict. Death was certainly an option. A jailer was called to keep watch. For anyone in Paul and Silas's situation, it would have been easy to lose hope and allow despair to set in. They were being punished for doing the right thing. But they refused to move into complaint and instead trusted God's ability to hear their prayers.

"*About midnight Paul and Silas were praying and singing hymns to God, and the other prisoners were listening to them*" (Acts 16:25). This part of the narrative astounds me each time I read it. Two men who had, through the power of Jesus, set a young girl free had been unjustly beaten and were bloody, bruised, and rejected. Yet they chose to pray and have a praise service amidst their dark and discomfort. Did they seriously find joy in this event?

The fact is, they weren't surprised by the suffering and the injustice. They knew it came with the territory of sharing the gospel of Jesus Christ. They were propelled by their relationship with Him and the power of His truth to transform lives. James says to "Count it all joy!" I have personally had to repent during disappointments and struggle for taking exception to this "recommendation," but Paul and Silas got it! They discovered the secret. They found no pleasure in the event, and they weren't waiting to feel happy. They had a focus fixed on the joy of their salvation and of their assignment. That joy partnered with faith to help them believe that there was more to accomplish for the Kingdom. This brought a profound contentment.

The other prisoners listened, and as their songs rose to Heaven, a violent earthquake shook the prison, the doors opened, and their chains fell off—not just for Paul and Silas, but all the prisoners! Can you imagine their joy in seeing that their freedom was a reality? It was a joy that was accompanied by relief and grateful enthusiasm. But when the jailer and his household were led to salvation, I expect everything in them exploded and joined with Heaven's celebration—it was the greater moment.

A Christian's joy is grounded in hope. Paul and Silas's testimony of radiant hope that released joy and praise in the darkest of moments prepared the atmosphere for deliverance, salvation, and revival. One thing we know—a life lived for the glory of God will have a joy that remains focused on who He is. That joy has the potential to minister to the needy world around us in ways that will amaze us!

O God, please instill in me the attitude of joy no matter what my circumstances. Remind me that joy can grow in me even when an event or situation is not causing me to feel pleasure. Thank you for the Holy Spirit, who is helping me to grow in this aspect of love each day. I declare that my hope is in you, and you have shown me in your Word that joy can be real!

The Practice of Joy

Day Twenty-Nine

Anxiety in a person's heart weighs him down, but an encouraging word brings him joy.

—Proverbs 12:25, NET)

The summer of 1988. Every radio station, my kids' t-shirts, signs on storefronts: "Don't Worry, Be Happy!" The song quickly reached #1 on the Billboard Hot Music 100 charts and remained there for weeks! The kids demanded I scroll through the stations on every car ride until I found it. Everyone everywhere was singing the words of Bobby McFerrin's song. It became the unofficial anthem in Jamaica after Hurricane Gilbert touched down that September. It lifted their spirits during one of the most devastating tragedies in the history of their island. There's something about the phrase "Don't worry, be happy!" that gives people "permission" to taste joy, even when it seems like they shouldn't.

In a way, Jesus gave the same command in His visit with Mary and Martha recorded in Luke 10. What may not be readily understood from the story, without some extra study, is that when Martha invited Jesus to her home that day, the Jewish people were celebrating "Sukkot," or "the season of our joy." During this seven-day holiday, the focus was joy! Small tents called "sukkahs" were erected for feasting and even sleeping. The festival commemorated the time in their history when the people of God dwelled in tents as they followed Him through the wilderness to the promised land. It was a time of celebrating God's "dwelling" with them—His presence! Luke describes the visit this way"

Experiencing Joy

And she had a sister called Mary, who sat at the Lord's feet and listened to his teaching. But Martha was distracted with much serving. And she went up to him and said, "Lord, do you not care that my sister has left me to serve alone? Tell her then to help me." But the Lord answered her, "Martha, Martha, you are anxious and troubled about many things, but one thing is necessary. Mary has chosen the good portion..."

—Luke 10:39–42a, ESV

Lori Wagner describes Martha as the "lady of the household" who would have been responsible for making sure guests were comfortable and well fed. But Jesus says to Martha that even though she's busy, there's only one thing needed—to be joyful about God's presence, as Jesus *is* the Emmanuel (God dwelling among us). It wasn't about her pulling off the perfect feast or being the perfect hostess. It was about reveling in the joy of spending time with Him.[6]

We all have busy schedules, distractions, bosses with deadlines, places to be, families that need feeding, laundry to fold, or cars that need gas. He knows! "Martha, Martha." Put your own name in here. "You are anxious about so many things! Have you forgotten I am here? That should be your focus in the many things, and it should bring you joy!" He is reminding Martha and us that the only truly important thing in the midst of the busyness is *joy*!

The practice of joy (we are all called to live and serve with joy) and the practice of presence (the mighty and powerful One dwells with us) are what being a follower of Jesus is all about. There will always be too many things to be done. There will always be struggle and sorrow. But there is joy to be found in relationship with Jesus. "Don't worry. Be happy!" Jesus is here! Experience the joy!

Jesus, today I rejoice that you are right here with me. Thank you for your welcome and your love as you call my name to remind me of your nearness. I worship you!

---

6 Adapted from https://sermons.com/sermon/lady-of-the-house-the-practice-of-joy/1492145. Access date: May 14, 2022.

Six Biblical Habits to Help Cultivate Joy

Day Thirty

Then our mouth was filled with laughter, and our tongue with shouts of joy; then they said among the nations, "The Lord has done great things for them."
—Psalm 126:2, ESV

During our thirty-day journey, we've learned that joy, a fruit of the Holy Spirit in our lives, often springs from viewing our everyday events and circumstances from eternity's perspective. With an intentional focus, we can experience His joy, knowing that He's in control. His joy is our strength, and He's at work in our lives. I think we're able to conclude from the testimonies shared here that more or greater biblical joy won't come from expanding our social media platform, accumulating earthly goods, or being promoted at work. We've seen that true biblical joy can't be stolen through loss, traffic delays, diagnoses, betrayals, infertility, old age, or rejection. Let's consider some practices that will continue to help us cultivate joy in our personal lives.

Worship

The psalmist David reminds his soul (Psalm 103) to bless the Lord in every circumstance. As he chooses to worship, he sets a course for every part of his being to enumerate, with gratitude and focus, the benefits of a Saviour who forgives, heals, redeems, and satisfies. This moves him to review the attributes of God, who is merciful, gracious, slow to anger, just, loving, and compassionate. As we worship the loving, gracious God who made a way for us to meet with Him, we begin to experience His joy.

> *You make known to me the path of life; in your presence there is fullness of joy...*
> —Psalm 16:11a, ESV

Obedience

Obedience to God's Word and ways is not always convenient or popular. It's much easier to sleep in on Sunday mornings than it is to get up for church. It's easier to skip a daily time with God than to carve it out as a priority. It's easier to follow the crowd than to stand alone because of your convictions. Obedience may cost us, but it liberates us. It yields to God, honouring who He is. Obedience releases joy.

> *If you keep my commandments, you will abide in my love ... These things I have spoken to you, that my joy may be in you, and that your joy may be full.*
> —John 15:10–11, ESV

Focus

The world around us has a way of spiritually blurring our vision. Problems seem like impossibilities, filling us with setbacks and defeat when our focus is off. With an unhindered and unclouded focus, we can look ahead—we can see morning beyond the night. It's laborious and confusing to see ahead if our eyes are riveted to the troubles of earth. There is something within us that is being called by eternity. That call should deliver a joy-filled hope.

> *fixing our eyes on Jesus, the pioneer and perfecter of faith. For the joy set before him he endured the cross...*
> —Hebrews 12:2a

Six Biblical Habits to Help Cultivate Joy

Gratitude

Joy flows from a grateful and responsive heart. Paul reminded the Thessalonians to rejoice always, to pray continually, and to give thanks in every situation. Recognize that life itself is a gift. Look to give joy to other people. Consider writing a gratitude journal, perhaps at the end of each day. Review the testimony of His goodness in your life. As a life is truly surrendered to God, there is a growing trust in God's goodness. As we come to know Him more, we cannot help but be grateful.

> *... giving thanks with joy to the Father. He made it so you could take part in the inheritance ... granted to God's holy people.*
> —Colossians 1:12, CEB

Forgiveness

One of the most powerful gifts you can ever give to yourself and others is forgiveness. You may have been rejected, overlooked, devalued, or betrayed. The forgiveness you give doesn't excuse the behaviour of those who hurt you, but it does prevent their behaviour from stealing your joy and destroying your heart. Forgiveness given to others sets you free to experience the strength of a fuller joy. We can't always communicate with our offender, but we can always communicate with God to settle accounts of the heart. Choose forgiveness to activate His joy.

> *What happiness for those ... forgiven! What joys ... What relief for those who have confessed their sins and God has cleared their record.*
> —Psalm 32:1–2, TLB

Giving

The research is clear. Joyful people give more at all levels—time, resources, attention, compassion, mercy. And the reverse is true. People who give of resources, love, mercy, benevolence, and time in loving and serving others are more joyful. For the Christian, this is a result of allowing the power of the Holy Spirit to work in one's life, making us more like Christ. Mother Teresa said "A joyful heart is the normal result of a heart burning with love. (The person) gives most who gives with joy."[7]

> *Each one must give as he has decided in his heart, not reluctantly or under compulsion, for God loves a cheerful giver.*
> —2 Corinthians 9:7, ESV

As a carrier of His joy, you have the potential to change atmospheres. Start incorporating these biblical habits today, and you'll be amazed at how readily your joy will be experienced and then released to share with others.

Take a few minutes to write your own prayer based on what God has spoken to you through these thirty days.

---

[7] Mother Teresa, *AZ Quotes*, https://www.azquotes.com/quote/408050 Last accessed 2022-05-18. Accessed May 20, 2022.

Small Group Helps

This devotional journey welcomes the participation of others in a small group setting, either in person or online. Each participant will need their own copy of the book and can journal any take-aways or questions from their daily readings. In a small group setting, all participants should be reading the devotional entries at the same time so that discussions centre around the same readings on any given week. Discussing your insights will reveal some impacting and exciting truths.

There are a variety of options for group reading. Choose a six-week session by reading the devotionals only on the five weekdays. Choose a five-week session by taking Sundays off. Choose a four-week session by having the group read one extra entry on week three and week four.

The group leader may select two to five questions from the following list for the weekly group meeting, which should run between sixty and eighty minutes. Vary your selection of questions from the list, adapting them to your group's focus. Be sure to allow time for personal thoughts, testimonies of growth, and any questions. Keep a scriptural view as foundational and expect God to meet with you as you gather. The preferred leadership style for this topic is facilitation, where the leader encourages both participation and time boundaries during sharing. The facilitator should be familiar with the material and keep the discussion moving.

Discussion Questions

(Choose Your Own Adventure!)

General questions for any week:

1. Which biblical character or event was most impactful to your growth this week?
2. What life lesson did you learn from that character or event?
3. Which testimony stood out for you this week? Share what you gained from it.
4. Share one truth from this week's readings that might be relevant to pass along to a specific friend for discussion in the future.
5. Choose a scripture verse from this week's devotionals and unpack what it means in your life right now.
6. Talk about your greatest joy challenge right now and pray for one another.

Questions specific to each day of the devotional readings:

Day One

1. Psalms 16:11 says that as I walk with the Lord, I know true joy and contentment. Where are the places you find true joy and contentment in your personal walk?
2. Today's prayer includes asking God to help you embrace the joy of simple things and familiar places. What are some things He's bringing to mind where you may have forgotten to take time for His joy?

Day Two

1. How is having the same love and being of one accord connected to the fulfilment of joy?
2. What are some relationships in your life that are helping to transform your walk?

Day Three

1. Share a time when you had an opportunity to lead someone to Jesus. Did you sense the joy of Heaven in that commitment they made?
2. What do you love about Betty's passion and how does it inspire you?

Day Four

1. Share with your group some thoughts about Jesus on the cross and how He could have had joy.
2. What is the basis of our joy regardless of what's going on around us? Explain what that means in your own life.

Day Five

1. What do you think was Chris's biggest downfall before he truly met Jesus and what does that speak to you?
2. What are some key choices that helped Chris come to understand true joy?

Day Six

1. Discuss how Sarah and Abraham found their joy.
2. How does God feel about laughter and why?

Day Seven

1. Every believer has the privilege of being used by God in effective intercession. How are you being used in this way?

Discussion Questions

2. If God knows the prayer of our hearts, why do we need to spend time telling Him?

Day Eight

1. Kayleigh went through one event that absolutely turned her life into a challenge she never anticipated. Has that ever happened to you and where was God in it?
2. Talk about the many ways in which God was present in Kayleigh's journey. Where are you seeing Him in your personal journey right now?

Day Nine

1. Imagine you'd been there when Jesus rode into Jerusalem. Share some of your thoughts about how that might have felt.
2. Where and how do you find times to raise your hosannas to the Lord?

Day Ten

1. How are joy and strength connected for you?
2. What part does gratitude play in helping you define joy?

Day Eleven

1. Christine faced a lot of misunderstanding about what life would look like if she came to Christ. How did God help her with the challenges?
2. What does it mean for you to live a surrendered life?

Day Twelve

1. How does a person find joy while waiting for someone they love to return to the Father?
2. What kind of party do you think the Father threw for you when you came into the kingdom?

Experiencing Joy

Day Thirteen

1. What kind of things do you think are trying to steal your joy in this particular season?
2. Summarize the story "The Luck of Roaring Camp" and a lesson it's meant to teach.

Day Fourteen

1. Psalm 95:1 tells us to sing for joy to the Lord and to shout joyfully to the rock of our salvation. How are you responding to that invitation?
2. What impressed you about Vanessa's choices?

Day Fifteen

1. Discuss the meaning of the night and the morning.
2. Have you ever entered a night when you've been waiting for the morning? Share a small part of your story.
3. How can you live with joyful expectation that morning is coming in your present circumstances or struggles?

Day Sixteen

1. After Stephen buried his mother, he felt overwhelmed, heartbroken, and depressed the very next day. Can this happen to Christians? Explain your answer.
2. What opportunities are you taking to spend time in His presence?

Day Seventeen

1. Have one of the card players in your group explain John's contribution.
2. Have some volunteers share one of the many scriptures in this contribution and unpack it for the group.

Discussion Questions

Day Eighteen

1. Have you ever had a time in your life when staying afloat seemed a greater priority than finding joy? Share with the group.
2. Ed and Lori had a journey that took much perseverance, faith, and support. At what places in the journey do you see Jesus as the way-maker for them?

Day Nineteen

1. How did joy interrupt Rhoda's task?
2. Chidi found his answer and turn around in worship. Have you ever had a similar experience? Share with the group.

Day Twenty

1. Share some of the numerous feelings Hannah must have had that day in the house of the Lord.
2. Talk about the secret to Hannah's strength.

Day Twenty-One

1. What are some laws of God through which obedience might bring you joy?
2. How does the life of Jesus model laws that are meant to bring us joy?

Day Twenty-Two

1. Lori said, "Perhaps I was more afraid than excited, but I was thanking God for not letting me miss what was clearly His path for me." What do you think she meant?
2. Why did Lori's joy seem hilarious to her?

Experiencing Joy

Day Twenty-Three

1. In some joy there is no element of selfishness—it is pure affection. It is intense, deep, breaking into song. How do we get to experience that kind of joy?
2. Share the name of someone God has placed in your life to share His great delight over you. Tell how that connects you to God.

Day Twenty-Four

1. Ryan says, "Think about it. If your mood—the emotional place that you find yourself in at any given moment—is the gatekeeper of joy in your life, you and I are both in for a rough journey ahead." What did he mean?
2. What would happen if you chose to change the way you view God's boundaries?

Day Twenty-Five

1. What is the "knowing" that Laura talks about?
2. Sometimes a tragic circumstance can release something from deep within that God uses to bringing healing and wholeness. Has it ever happened for you? Share with your group.

Day Twenty-Six

1. A generous lifestyle begins with the recognition of who God is. Share some principles in God's kingdom that help us to understand the value and joy of living a lifestyle of generosity.
2. Identify someone who has modeled the generosity of the gospel for you and share how that impacted your life.

Day Twenty-Seven

1. Chat with your group about the importance of prayer and blessing over the young.

Discussion Questions

2. Discuss the truth of Melissa's joy statement, "It is shareable and transferrable."

Day Twenty-Eight

1. Paul and Silas were being punished for doing the right thing. But they refused to move into complaint and instead trusted God's ability to hear their prayers. Talk about how you might respond in such a challenge.

Day Twenty-Nine

1. Explain the invitation that Jesus was giving Martha.
2. What busyness is challenging His invitation to joy in your life?

Day Thirty

1. Have some volunteers share the prayer they've written if they are comfortable doing so.
2. For which one of the habits will you most likely be asking God's help?

Contributors

 Vanessa Brobbel, a veteran homeschool mom and artist from the Niagara region, works alongside her husband, Floyd, for a mission called The Voice of the Martyrs. For the past twenty-one years, she has spoken at conferences and women's retreats across Canada. This ministry purposes to create an awareness of the persecution levelled against Christians around the world while actively providing tools to mentor the body of Christ both domestically and internationally to grow through adversity.

Friends describe Vanessa as a beautiful soul with a natural teaching gift. She loves her family dearly and the work that she does for VOM. Warm, caring, passionate, artistic, and full of joy are just a few words to describe this amazing woman!

VOMC
vomcanada.com

Trouble on the Way
store.vomcanada.org/category/all/books/vomc-originals/trouble-on-the-way

Melissa Bone is an ordained minister, author, and speaker. She lives in Grimsby, Ontario with her husband, Terry, where they served as the Senior Pastoral Couple at Lakemount Worship Centre for over ten years.

Melissa has written and co-written several books, including *"The Family Blessing Guidebook"* and a devotional book for women based on the women of Luke and Acts, entitled *"Luke's Ladies."*

With a lifelong commitment to mentoring the next generation, Melissa inspires and champions women to see them raised up and released into their God-given destinies. She is trained in birth coaching (labour doula) and chaplaincy and works in hospitals, assisting both practically and pastorally.

Melissa enjoys mentoring her three adult children and their families, along with her seven grandchildren.

Born as number five in a family of seven children, Betty Chisholm has always been curious and adventurous. As a pre-schooler, an early fascination with fire left her tottering between life and death. Having journeyed through a lifetime of medical interventions, shame, abortion, and a broken marriage, Betty stands a trophy of God's grace, healing, and redemptive plan. She is an ordained minister with OBFF (Ministers Network Canada) and has served as founder and director of Prison Revival Ministries for thirty-five years. Her ministry has included Music with a Mission, a local Aglow presidency, international missions, speaking, and media interviews.

Betty has written her story in book form entitled *"Out of the Flame."* A mother, grandmother, and retired career hairdresser, Betty's prayer is that her transparency in relating her journey will bring hope and freedom to others. Betty and her husband, John, reside in St. Catharines, Ontario.

Contributors

Chris Collins grew up in Hamilton, Ontario and attended Mohawk College and later Tyndale University. From a very young age, Chris developed a passion for music. He has been a vocalist, choir member, trumpet player, and has marched with the drum and bugle corps. He served as full-time director for the corps for four years, taught vocal music at a local church school, and now serves his local church in the areas of worship, prayer, and ministry eldership.

Chris has a heart for people. Having found his way back to the Lord following a deep depression, he understands the needed role of the body of Christ to walk in compassion and support. Chris often finds unique ways to bring people together, providing both friendship and small group leadership.

Chris married his beautiful wife, Nancy, in 2000, and they reside in Beamsville, Ontario. Apparently, he is mildly interested in football, and in his spare time, you're most likely to find him on the local golf course or off on a long country drive with his wife.

Dr. John Courtney, a graduate of EPBC, ordained in 1972, received his BRS degree from Mennonite Brethren Bible College (CMU) in 1980. John continued to pursue studies at Winnipeg Theological Seminary (MMin) and Providence (MA), receiving a Doctor of Divinity, honoris causa from Providence College and Theological Seminary in 2011.

He has recently retired from a forty-seven-year run at his lifelong passion as Executive Director of Youth for Christ, Winnipeg, serving over 11,000 youth annually. While John has been the recipient of numerous prestigious awards, including the Queen's Diamond Jubilee medal, he has remained humble, engaged, and mission-focused with a heart to see youth become life-long Christ-followers. He presently mentors leaders globally in his new international YFC "retirement" position.

A two-time cancer survivor with an amazing testimony of God's healing grace, John enjoys a vibrant and active family life with his fantastic wife of fifty years, Susan, their three sons, spouses, and eight grandkids.

Christine Dobrocky calls Niagara, Ontario home, where she was born and raised in a family with two older brothers. Her Roman Catholic upbringing contributed to her hunger for God in her adult life. Her lived experience battling an eating disorder, being a former fitness competitor, being a police officer, a resulting PTSD diagnosis, and a suicide attempt were driving forces that led her on a path to healing in her late twenties. At thirty-six, she decided to surrender her life to God and has never looked back.

Christine enjoys a holistic lifestyle that encompasses regular exercise, time in nature, and meditation. Some of her passions include reading, writing, riding a motorcycle, serving her church community, and helping others better understand the positive impacts that living a Christian life can have.

To learn more about Christine and to read her blog, visit Christinedobrocky.ca

Kayleigh Duggan was born in the Niagara Region, Ontario. When she started high school, she moved with her parents overseas as a missionary kid for four years, spending two years in Kenya and two years in Tanzania. While there, Kayleigh served with the worship team and the children's ministry. Upon return, she started a fantastic internship at her local church, Lakemount Worship Centre. During the second year of the program, she added to her studies a course load from Portland Bible College, Oregon, that would take her on a journey toward her Bachelor of Theology.

Following what could have been a life-altering illness, she is now pressing toward her goal of graduating from these studies and stepping in to serve the body of Christ in a pastoral role. She uses her spare time to flip burgers or take cash at Wendy's, curl up with a good book, tackle a challenging puzzle, or hang out with family and friends.

Contributors

Ryan Harmon serves on the pastoral team at Lakemount Worship Centre in Grimsby, Ontario. He's involved with the young adult's ministry (LYA), Alpha Course, the worship team, and Sunday serve teams. Ryan is passionate about seeing people, young *and* old, encounter the life-changing presence of Jesus Christ through the preaching of the Word. He loves to read and travel, is crazy about sports, and is just about always down to do something adventurous. Ryan and his beautiful wife, Jenna, are living their best lives in the Niagara region, where they're raising two beautiful boys, Moses and Shepard.

During Ed and Lori McKay's thirty-three years of marriage, they've been passionate about serving both in the local church and on mission. In 2002, they began ministry with Next Level International in short-term missions, church planting, and leadership training programs to Eastern Europe. They also started fostering children and eventually adopted their son, Dee, now twenty-five and married.

They have pastored in PAOC churches in Echo Bay and Smithville, Ontario, and have served in missions to Peru and Barbados. Lori has been a very successful career bookkeeper/administrator in various mission agencies and within her community. Ed has assisted the Salvation Army in their care ministry to those in need. Whether in itinerant ministry, preaching, teaching, or leading worship (supported by his wife), Ed shares his passion for both the Word and people. Lori and Ed strongly value relationships and love investing in small groups and prayer gatherings to build the Kingdom. Ed and Lori live in Simcoe, Ontario.

Experiencing Joy

Chidi Opara grew up as a pastor's kid in Nigeria, serving alongside his father in almost every church ministry area as needed. He came to Canada in 2004, where his educational pursuits included Niagara College, a degree from McMaster University, and an MBA from Brock University in Data Analytics. Following eleven years as an IT Client Analyst for the city of St. Catharines, he currently serves Niagara Health as a Senior Decision Support Performance Advisor.

Chidi's ministry has included First Baptist Church, Welland and Royal House, St. Catharines in areas of worship, media, and young adults. He presently serves his home church, Lakemount Worship Centre, in worship, media, and prayer. His passion for God and his welcoming smile are infectious!

Chidi married his wife, Ola, in 2010, and they are blessed with three beautiful children: Joshuana, David, and Christabel. As a family they love workouts, sports, game and movie nights, and playground picnics. Chidi also enjoys playing the guitar and connecting people with the power of scripture. He thrives in organizing events, building, IT projects, and gardening.

With humility of heart and obedience to the leading of the Spirit, Laura Woodley Osman loves to serve the body of Christ. She has been a worship leader and singer/songwriter for many years, spreading God's love internationally. Her most recent CD, *Four Winds*, is a collection of songs to encourage and prepare hearts for Jesus' return. Laura has four other records: *Home, In Love, Invisible Realms,* and *Story of All Stories*. She has also authored a children's book and developed a biblically-based fragrance. Laura has the heart of a psalmist and loves being her Heavenly Daddy's girl.

Since 2006, Laura has walked with her husband, Daniel, in both marriage and ministry. They adore their kids: Noah (2011), Nathan (2012), and Grace (2014). Together they share a love for God's Word and His people. More than anything, they love seeing God's kingdom released wherever they go!

www.spiritsoulbody.com

Joy Slaughter, better known as Madame Jwa by her Haitian friends, spent eighteen wonderful years serving and raising up leaders in the organization "Love Haiti," which she co-founded. The vision of the ministry, continued now by the locals, is to "Rescue, Restore, and Edify" by offering humanitarian aid and sharing a message of revival and transformation.

In 2012 she married her husband, well-known musician Alvin Slaughter, and together they have traversed North America bringing the joy of Jesus. As a Certified Clinic Hemodialysis Technician, she presently works with end-stage renal patients full-time, giving them dialysis treatments, while also training others at the treatment centre. Joy resides in Buffalo, New York, where her heart's passion and compassion find expression in ministering hope, healing, and inspiration within her community. Friends describe Joy as a lover of Jesus, full of laughter and encouragement, who exemplifies what it means to live life to the full.

www.facebook.com/joyslaughter2012

Lori Webster's home has always been Ontario, with the exception of the adventure featured in this devotional. Having spent her most formative years in Sudbury and on Manitoulin Island, she especially feels at home in a landscape of birch trees and rocks. She has worked in various counselling positions and, most recently, has been assisting newcomers to Canada to settle successfully.

Lori enjoys serving in prayer, Rapha healing ministry, and Trauma Healing Groups in her much-loved home church. She has served on several life-changing short-term mission trips to Guatemala, St. Lucia, Slovakia, and Turkey. While being an introvert who will never get through her book list, she also enjoys laughter and fun shared with family and friends. Lori has a sneaking suspicion that God is not finished with His surprise adventures in His good plan for her life!

 Stephen Wesley BTh was born on an army base in Northern Ontario, raised in Germany, and educated in America, where he earned his Bachelor of Theology Degree. He was launched into full-time ministry in Uganda, East Africa. Stephen has been in ministry for thirty plus years and brings an international and seasoned perspective, having served the body of Christ in many capacities and ministered in many nations. He functions in areas of teaching, prophetic and pastoral giftings, and is a well-known and regular conference speaker. Stephen is a course writer for TheosU and is an author of two books, *Cornerstone Truths for the Christian Life* and *Growth and Maturity*.

Stephen is a joy-filled, anointed communicator of the Word of God. Along with his wife, Angela, they have founded Beyond Borders Ministries. Stephen serves his local church, Lakemount Worship Centre in Grimsby in the areas of prayer ministry and teaching and as an extension of the local church as a Partnering Ministry.

beyond-borders.ca

About the Author

Ruth Teakle lives with her husband, Carl, in Beamsville, Ontario. She loves to spend time with her three children and their spouses and her eleven grandchildren. Although retired, Ruth serves as a support staff member at Lakemount Worship Centre in Grimsby, Ontario, where she previously served on full-time and part-time staff for eighteen years. Her roles varied from overseeing small groups and missions to prayer and pastoral care. As well, she has led and assisted with numerous short-term missions to the Caribbean, Eastern Europe, Ukraine, South America, northern Ontario, and Quebec.

On the home front, Ruth and Carl have fostered over 130 children during a twenty-five-year period. Ruth has worked within the Correctional Services of Canada, volunteered with numerous summer camp programs through both Girls Guides of Canada and the Salvation Army, directed an annual city-wide Christmas toy program, and filmed a national training course for telephone prayer partners. She also served for many years in local, area, and national capacities with Aglow International Canada prior to pastoral ministry.

Ruth's academic pursuits have included studies at Lakeshore Teachers' College, Brock University (Bachelor of Arts), and Wagner University (Master of Practical Ministries). She has completed ESL studies and is a Certified Anger Management Specialist and Trauma Healing Training Facilitator.

Prior to taking additional Religious Studies courses with Global University in preparation for ordained ministry, Ruth enjoyed a successful thirty-two-year career as an elementary school teacher.

Ruth's heart is to see people become passionate followers of Christ who walk in wholeness and in the fullness of their destinies. She has a strong sense of mission to help people build healthy connections with God and others. Her challenging but victorious personal journey makes her well qualified to share on Heaven's plan for us to experience joy in our personal journeys.

Additional Note: Ruth's first devotional, *Changing Seasons*, is a pocket/purse sized devotional full of encouragement from God's Word written especially for seniors, and it's one of the GODQUEST SERIES available only through The Bible League, Canada. bibleleague.ca/resources/godquest/.

Pursuing Patience, Pursuing Peace, Choosing Love, Choosing Kindness, and *Cultivating Faith* are available through Word Alive Press and numerous national and international outlets.

Ruth has also authored a delightfully illustrated children's book for children ages four to nine, *Joshua Wonders: What Does the Tooth Fairy Do with My Teeth?* available through numerous national and international outlets.

www.ingramcontent.com/pod-product-compliance
Lightning Source LLC
Chambersburg PA
CBHW070207100426
42743CB00013B/3085